Tzimtzum

Tzimtzum

5 contemporary poets lend us their hearts

Abeyta · Arness · Broderick
Hill · Seluja

Mercury HeartLink
www.heartlink.com

Tzimtzum: *5 contemporary poets lend us their hearts*
Copyright ©2013 Mercury HeartLink

ISBN: 978-0-9892882-4-8
Publisher: Mercury HeartLink, www.heartlink.com
Printed in the United States of America

Cover photograph: Corinna Stoeffl
http://stoefflphotography.com

Contact individual authors at:
    Aaron A. Abeyta, aaabeyta@adams.edu
    Tani Arness, tani.arness@gmail.com
    Richard Broderick, richb@lakecast.com
    Judyth Hill, rockmirth@cybermesa.com
    Katherine DiBella Seluja, www.katherineseluja.com

TANI ARNESS

We Do Not, Yet, Know How to Pray   *7*

Shape Shifting   *9*

Numbers   *10*

Grandma Told Me Once,   *12*

Studying Beauty   *13*

Sexy   *15*

It Is a Day of Half Light   *16*

Arctic Land Bridge   *18*

December Train Into Philly   *19*

Tower of Babel   *21*

Work   *23*

Winter Solstice   *24*

Mud, Sky, Lithograph   *26*

The Day   *28*

In Your Bones   *29*

Whale Hunting   *31*

Tell Me Your Day   *32*

Water   *33*

Time Dilation   *35*

Dorcas   *37*

RICHARD BRODERICK

Listening to a CD of Glenn Gould
    Performing "The Goldberg Variations"   45

All Present And Accounted For   46

Autumn Tutorial   48

Night Shift   49

Cote de Valais   50

Every River   51

Between the Covers   52

Song of the Fat Woman Swimming off Cocoa Beach   53

Boys Fishing   54

Swimming Laps   55

August Sunset from the Highest Point in St. Paul   56

The Boxing Lesson   57

Upon Receiving My Brother's Ashes   58

On the Highway to Heaven   59

Jesus of Walmart   61

The Long Drive Down   63

Dichos   64

Dark Day   67

KATHERINE DIBELLA SELUJA

Blue Vase   77

Dehiscence   78

You will find it in the stillness   80

When I think of birth   82

Vena Cava Fable   84

Upon hearing that an Uruguayan mother
        fed her children grass   86

Santuario   87

You in 'Burque   89

These words for my daughters   90

No Storm Like Him   91

You would have to be Adirondack green mountains   93

Pantoum for Greystone Locked Ward   94

Telephone, 4 a.m.   96

Spinning with Thorazine   98

You were picturing a '68 Mustang   99

Delirium tremens   101

Conversing with Cirrhosis   102

News of a Brother's Death   103

Of calamine and honey   104

AARON A. ABEYTA

the fragile vessel	111
love poem after a passing antelope	112
a true love poem	115
brown inca beside a river	117
cartographer's love poem	118
man falls from great distance writes poem	120
Ricky (still) loves Lulu	123
if we never met	126
as my love speaks	129
1,017,900 pounds	131
two lions hunted the plains of africa	133
the seven stars visible	137
the earth at night your body	138
for centuries and so on	141
the calculus of you	144
two rivers next to which i would love you and how	148
i have for a moment	150
love poem on stone	152
teeter	153
like hermes at the edge of a field	154
touch and voice	156
good friday	157
crane poem for my love	160
the fisherman's song of despair or *oncorhyncus mykiss*	165

JUDYTH HILL

This Will Find You Ready   177

Mermaid Dreaming Fish Into Diatonic Scales   179

Thirst Is For Knowing Water   181

First Steps   183

How I Got Here   185

Night of River's Filling: A Crown of Sonnets   187

Gift Event   191

Here is Your Scarab,   192

Map to (W)holy Here   194

Don't Travel, Journey!   198

StudioOnlySymbolHearsWindDesire   200

Ritual for the Wild Love Moon   202

Everything Is In Front Of Us   203

Love's Offices   205

Oficinas del amor   207

Wisteria Mantra   209

Startled Solstice   210

Wear the Ring of the New   212

WAGE PEACE   214

Last Time   216

Author Bios   219

COMMENTARY — OH THESE POETS

We don't know who we'll become next in this mind/body, on this home planet, in what we call the manifest future. There is a striving here, and a shaping of patterns, then more solid forms like thoughts arrive and all that they create. The maker of days seems to be expanding with us, and we with her. There is awareness, and an increasing suspicion that our participation is directly involved in this unfoldment, *is* this unfoldment. We ponder: Perhaps every thing is connected brilliantly, forever, and we wonder if fear as we've known it could become obsolete.

Changes viewed through the lens of time are occurring at an expediential rate as the life-force shifts from state to state. A lot of people call that change death, and think of it only in terms of how it looks when a form has outgrown its usefulness, forgetting that that energy is being regenerated elsewhere, elsewhen. Sometimes there's grief; sometimes it's good riddance. In my lifetime a combination of force, reason and material production has become the bad guy—a paradigm on its way out, or better yet, the rhythm of a pendulum reaching its apex to turn just in time toward the other end. Sure, it'll get messy.

But the new poetics can embrace a new science, and the machine can be programmed to understand that relatedness and love are paramount to survival. Beauty still rules, and the poet listens for these cues, for the indicators of new pathways. A point with no dimension—but let's say it's the size of a universe—has been cleared like a meadow deep in the forest. A ceremony has begun to unite that which thought itself separate. The poets have arrived—each with their own language of magickal implements. If you think this sounds far out, stick around. The earth just might be a kingdom of heaven, and everything you think you see happening, is happening the way you think you see it. Imagine!

—Stewart S. Warren, 2013
Editor and publisher, *Mercury HeartLink*

Tzimtzum

TANI ARNESS

And yet, there is only
One great thing,
The only thing.
To live and see in huts and on journeys
The great day that dawns,
And the light that fills the world.

—Song recorded from a group of the Kitlinuharmiut (Copper Eskimo),
as written by Knud Rasmussen in The Report of the Fifth Thule
Expedition 1921-1924.

Tani Arness

I write as a spiritual practice, which is to say a practice of living. In order to keep writing, I have to surrender my ego and open my heart and mind over and over again to the shy and fitful creative process. I have to pay attention to what is flowing through me and get rid of my preconceived notions about the type of writer I think I *should* be. Some days this is a struggle and some days a gift. My best writing comes from an "other" realm and can heal and transform. There are not a lot of things I know, but I have come to know that creativity gives purpose to my life. It helps guide me forward. If I am not practicing creativity daily then I am not happy.

Serious writers love to talk about discipline and I think a certain amount of discipline, or focus and follow through, is necessary. However I guard against a driven approach to achieving a quick product or image of "success." I find that too much push in that direction creates, in me, a fatigue, and the resulting product becomes more of a mental gymnastics. This kind of productivity can be entertaining but ultimately does not move me, or my readers, to a deeper level of living.

Years ago, as part of my own commitment to my creativity, I completed studies for a Master's degree in creative writing. I continue to be grateful for that time of focus and study. I also feel that, in many ways, I had to recover from the drive and focus I learned in that program. While I enjoy reading a poem closely and learning from that poem, I avoid the analytical debates about what makes a good poem in favor of a more intuitive approach. I believe that poetry is particularly fragile for the grasping hands of academia. I believe that turning poetry into too much of a disciplined, measured mental exercise kills the spirit of a poem. Any creative endeavor thrives with a mix of structure and knowledge as well as an open heart and freedom. I strive to stay in the spiritual space of freedom. I write for myself first and, when

I decide to send my poems out into the world, I hope they speak simply enough to our humanity; I hope they add beauty and insight to the lives of readers.

In my mind, all meaningful creativity requires a certain amount of "inspiration," yet poetry requires even a gentler touch than prose because poetry seeks only the essence of the thing. There is no "fill-in" allowed. I must be listening very carefully in order to hear the lines and not to add any weight that does not belong there. A poem doesn't need to be organized to carry plot or result in resolution, it must be light enough to take flight.

I relate to poetry not just as a writer or practitioner but also as a lover of poetry. I appreciate the many styles and forms of poetry and performance of poetry. Poetry has given me the gift of wonderful new friends and social events, entertainment and laughter, playfulness and tears, beauty and healing. As more of an introvert, one of my favorite ways to experience poetry is to sit alone and read poems quietly on my couch, or sit with a few close friends and read poems aloud to each other. In these moments, some poems feel transcendent. Reading a transcendent poem offers a prayer-like connection; it offers, often, wisdom and solace. A transcendent poem, to me, is not a certain style or theme. It may tell a story, sing a lullaby, or tantalize with whimsy. Such poems have given me new experiences, have changed the way I see. Such poems have made me feel less alone, made me feel more a part of the human experience. Poems continue to give to me.

Thus, as a teacher of poetry, my number one hope is to help students fall in love with poetry and with the expansive art of their own self-expression. I appreciate the layers of meaning that can be unveiled when one "studies" a poem. I also appreciate the pure experience of just letting a poem "wash over" you—an experience of sound and image, connected or disparate threads of story and meaning, feeling and image. First things first. I strive to offer up the power, beauty and creative process of poetry. I thrive on reaching out to people who have no idea they could love poetry. I work to help create a safe place, and many different starting places, for students to play, experiment and take risks in expressing themselves—for students to look inward and listen for what is echoing around there. Just like in life, a writer/reader must first fall in love with a thing, then there is plenty of time to work out the finer points of give and take.

Poetry can be a calling for some and not for others, but I do not see poetry as a niche art. I am uplifted by the long history of poetry thriving in every culture that has ever existed. I believe the art of words is broad enough to have something to offer us all, and to have room for us all! Sometimes it takes some digging to find a poem that you can really love! Sometimes you have to sit down and write/speak it yourself. It is always worth it. It is always an opening. There is no better gift than the right poem at the right time!

—Tani Arness

We Do Not, Yet, Know How to Pray

I.
We do not know anything but the stories—
the sacrificial fires, the stone-sharpened blades,
the drunken orgies inside of large, desert tents—
We hold our children in our arms while they cry,
and we don't know how to call our misgivings,
how to explain the wrong parts to the children.

II.
Sometimes women say nothing,
because we do not, yet, know how to pray.
And we must cross the river.

III.
And so the right words wait beneath our tongues
while the earth pulls us, keeps us from drifting skyward.
We wrap long roads around our feet
so that we can carry with us the many large
cities we stepped in.
We speak of the places without mentioning their gods.

IV.
We concentrate on the snaking roads ahead.
We try to remember the words from the old, leather books.
We tell the children, *Once upon a time* . . .
Sometimes we leave the scary parts out.

V.
About the terrifying stories of lions with long teeth and claws,
the children are tickled with glee to feel danger. We let the children run
       freely
in and out of doors and stories. They run from it, they come back. They
play together, pretending their sudden deaths and salvations.

VI.
We are carrying the first things
we picked up—
our love letters, our children, our favorite clay pots,
we stand on one side of the river, waiting—

VII.
The problem is the stories
are all so far away—
until yesterday, at the river,
which didn't "part" exactly
but evaporated to within inches of mud.

VIII.
Usually we women will carry only as much as we can carry
without breaking. But sometimes
we lift hearts heavy as our children lost in the hills.
Sometimes we wake from dreams
and get up and run as far as we can to the east.
Sometimes the spirits of the dawn see us
and they answer our questions by dropping bread from heaven.

SHAPE SHIFTING
1 Corinthians 12:7-11

Not a shape shifter, I have never dreamt
that I am a grain of sand, or a billion grains of sand,
or a bird or a tiger. But I am told
some people dream these things, and I think it must be nice.
In my dreams, always, I am me,
though I can call out, and, sometimes, a white tiger comes—
I can't say if she desires fighting or protection.

Is this what Jesus meant
walking around in those sandals those two thousand years ago
talking about Holy Spirit and the seven gifts?
Oh, how, as a child, I wanted one of those gifts!
I studied the thin, gold-rimmed pages, the lists:
prophecy, wisdom, tongues, interpretation of tongues,
teaching, service, and miracles . . .

But I don't remember hearing about
the gift of the grain of sand
the gift of tigers
or the gift of birds.
Yes, so many forgotten—
the gift of rivers, the gift of trees,
the gift of sun and soil and bees . . .

Not a shape shifter, not a man and then a god,
I am told, The Raven Stole the Sun.
I am told that dreams sometimes come true:
sand, and tigers, and birds.
I am told that God is in me.

Numbers

66 books, 1,189 chapters, 40,000 verses,
28 of which I memorized one young summer,
at least 12 of which I knew in song.
150 times I am told that the Lord spoke to Moses.
8 times Balaam, the pagan diviner, whispered oracles.
6—the beast. 7—God's lucky number.
Infinity—the child's spiritual confusion
because everything read like fact
yet nothing changed—no mountains moving,
no camels or needles or pearly gates, no 7 angels with trumpets or seals;
women weren't even covering their heads
in the houses of the Lord.
And so the number of years became factored into
the percentage of holy and unholy truth.
For 3 years, I had to close my eyes and count to 10
before I could sleep, because the devil worked in mysterious ways.
I had to keep track of the 7 gifts of the Holy Spirit,
the 6 days of creation, and the 100,000 reasons for *right*.
Wrong just lurked out there, a big 0, the wind.
I had 24 hours a day, 10,080 minutes a week to
count my blessings, count my faith, my witnessings, my omissions.
I can't count how many times I committed the sin of doubt,
doubting love and will and destiny, and the sin of fear.
I can't count how many times I knew God,
and how many times I didn't know anyone.
40 years wandering in the desert—
how many blessings, and how many times wrath?
I can't count how many generations it takes to link
God's apples and snakes—

Studying Beauty

She's beautiful, he says, I mean she's gorgeous!
What does that mean? I ask him.
Taken aback, he pauses—
I just mean she's an attractive woman, that's all.
Oh, because you said it like it's a fact rather than feeling,
like maybe there is some irrefutable quality that makes her attractive.

Well, he says, you have to admit, by most standards,
she would be considered pretty.
I suppose, I say, wondering.
You're just acting jealous.
Be serious. Don't you see her big, bright eyes,
full lips, smooth skin, long, thick hair,
long legs, perfectly shaped ass? . . .
I'm not sure I see what you see, I say.

I stare, imagining her in dingy clothes, no makeup, bad haircut . . .
Would she still be beautiful?

I attempt to gauge the cost of her
waxing, shopping, high-heeled boots, subtle mineral makeup . . .
And how much would it cost me to invest in such an idea.
And to what end?
Am I symmetrical? Is my face the right shape, my hips? my breasts? . . .

I've been studying beauty my whole life and I still can't figure it out.
I see trend and style, painted and not painted.

Rigid, curved and slumped.
I see shadow and light. I even see sadness and hiding.
I want to agree with him, Yes she is, she's gorgeous,
but somehow it doesn't seem fair to make such delineations.
I can't find that thing that makes a woman not beautiful.

SEXY

"You should wear something that makes you feel sexy," he said to me.
He doesn't understand
I cannot just go to my closet
and put on heels or a tight black dress to feel sexy.

I feel sexy in hiking boots on rocky mountain trails.
I feel sexy in African cloth and drums and pounding dance.
I feel sexy when I'm strong like that,
when I feel my own power in my own body and I don't need anyone.

And I feel sexy when I'm soft and safe,
wrapped in bright, flowing cotton skirts,
stepping with bare feet across warm, grassy fields;
I feel sexy wearing grass and rain.

I feel sexy when I'm standing at the ocean, looking on the inside
and finding so many gods there.
I feel sexy when the sky is big and I am small, irrelevant
except for my breath mingling with falling stars.

I feel sexy when I'm touching him and he is touching me,
when our fingertips read our bodies' Braille,
and we draw maps to places we have never been—
his hands on me, warm sensation of being alive.

I feel sexy when I'm wearing the earth,
dirt beneath my back, the sun warming bare skin,
the sky like a mirror overhead reflecting my
blue breath and wisps of sigh. . .

It Is a Day of Half Light

Look outward to the swells
of waves. From where

orchids cannot survive the freeze
but hillsides are brushed with frenzy of fireweed.

Think of history as magnificence
and robed explorers in cargo ships

unloading polished wood and tin
in the blowing sand of people gathering on beach shores.

Whole villages decimated
by flu.

One white stone on the hill marks the history of one harpoon
fired through the white man's door.

Does anyone know how to step across some small piece of ocean?
Land bridges have formed corridors

between continents—though really just one woman
standing where the sun sets loving, of course, one man standing
    where it rises.

The paddle scrapes against shallow river stone,
pushes a wooden rowboat into fish camp.

Children run alongside the travel of riverbanks
and laugh at the games of water against earth.

Elders used to tell stories
that pulled the ruins up the beach, the river to the far side.

One's voice can get lost in a time—
small pieces of bone wash up on the shore.

Does anyone know how to step across
some small piece of ocean?

Arctic Land Bridge

I could step out of his small aluminum boat
onto his long shore of old houses,
black rock, and sand dunes, tundra ponds and loon eggs.

But what if, in April's thaw, the underground spring of me
started breaking up
into the thin needles of ice, *niloruqs*, scooped up
and carried home in buckets?

What if I touched his whitening sky, him, born dawn—
and beaten back into winter again and again?

What if I was meant to be a ghost in a long white dress
except the correct stars were misplaced in the sky?

What if he was meant to be the balance between one
heavy side and the other,
but was born in a village tipped sideways?

When the door of him flies open,
he is a scared bird caught in a chimney. When the door of him
opens he is a raven strong against the snowdrifts.

I recognize the oldest place in me,
the deep sea, the core of the mountain
that wants him.

    Niloruqs is spelled phonetically from the word used in Wales, Alaska
    for the shattered needles of spring ice.

December Train Into Philly

There are cities built like ladders toward heaven.
In earth, there are tunnels with streaks of light blazing through darkness,
and there are platforms crowded with people wrapped in wallets
        and cell phones.
And I am just like them, the anonymous crowds, yet I feel so
far away and untouchable through the windows of trains.
Unsure if I am more or less of myself as the conductor leans in,
"Next Stop. Haverford."

The winter is dark and full of spindly trees and the rain
will soon begin to seep through my new leather boots.
And they say we'll only remember a handful of days from our lives.
The other thousands disappear into silent routine.
Outside my window, I make a conscious effort to see something:
That woman is wearing a red hat;
she has a faraway look, as if she wants to ask me,
What is the difference between angels and trees?

I pull out my train ticket, whizzing forward.
Black train tracks push through towns of forest and hill.
Each rail and tie pulls us toward the same destination
where rain-blackened streets and tall city buildings will reach down
and press us closer together.
Out the window, lines of track appear in front of us. Glistening.
I ride the tracks like a prayer toward what I hope exists.
Each click and sway sings, Please God, please . . .
Over river and horizon, silhouettes of light etch humanity
in twinkles and squares. I

imagine this equals love . . .
What will I become after this day disappears into all the others?
Soon I will step out of the train station, again, into the winter rain.

Tower of Babel
Genesis 11:1-9

We were building a staircase to heaven,
a square base with sloping, stepped sides leading upward.
(Who hasn't wanted such a ladder?)
But the Lord said,
Then nothing they plan
will be impossible for them . . .
and he pulled it down.

The whole world had one language;
we spoke moon and antelope, stars and rivers—
and then there was a confusion of strange
vowels and clickings on our tongues—
we spoke without hearing words.

The Lord scattered us
over the earth
and we stopped building
towers to God,
and we started building
roads back to each other.
Lovers, unable to silence their desire,
whispered sweet nothings, rolling R's and swooning vowels,
into each other's ears,
and another language was born of lips and tongue.

I, too, wanted to find what was invisible,
that place where nothing is impossible.
I, too, baked bricks in the sun,

fastened them together with tar,
carefully placed each piece beneath heaven, constructing my destiny.
And I watched as God scattered it all.

Perhaps destiny is not the right word,
and ambition is not from God.
Maybe there is something better to build than towers.
Maybe only language overcomes separation
even between heaven and earth.
Perhaps words are meant to be indecipherable prayers,
and God is just the wind.
Scattered. God scattered our hearts.

Work

In America, we have *workrooms* and *workout rooms*
and *individual work spaces* and people say we should
know what our *work is* . . .

And I keep thinking of that white American man
who landed in an Amazon village
and just sat there for like two years
while everyone else was planting corn and building houses
and sweeping floors and cooking for the children . . .
And, finally, he wanted to plant himself a row of corn too.

I think that is what our real work is.
It is the craving that comes, when we are not too tired to feel it,
for the satisfaction of doing what needs to be done.
It is the turquoise song that rises in our throats when
we get back that desire to fill our days with living.

Winter Solstice

He says, *You are the sound of cranes overhead.*

"But I can't fly," I say, "I can't stay in formation.
Some days winter is just more winter
and I can't spend one more minute in the grocery store line."
I can't stand for one second more in this pile of leaves
without a pirouette, *plié*, up and spin. Away.

He says, *Yes, darkness embeds itself into the soles of feet, like a splinter.*

But I can't see, not even one small stamen of spirit.
I can't stand up and breathe with all of this darkness outside
and blue trapped only round the moon.
I say, "I just want to watch Jackie Chan movies."

He says, *The crane lands on a billion particles of sand.*

But I've never stood on a snow mound whistling to the Northern Lights.
I've never even said thank you to the frogs
who stood post at the pond outside my window.
I say, "I can't."

He remembers, *One small splinter of stone which is white.*

"I can't."

He insists, *I adore you Gleaming Winter.*

I pirouette, *plié*, up, kick and spin. Away.

I call back to him—"Thank you six-foot wingspan, Escher birds.
Thank you unimbedded Love. Forgive me, my beauty, cold and impatient,
my secret winter animal, my soft body, crying.
Thank you, and I fly away from you, and I go now. Goodbye."

He says, *Remember*—

I call to him, "Goodbye. Good bye cold, yellow winter sun.
Goodbye charcoal scratching, charcoal shadowing beneath my eyes.
Goodbye dark fields of sand, under my feet, in my ears, on the moon
—Dear Winter—Please. Do not follow me. Goodbye."

*Quotes from "Images," *Technicians of the Sacred*, edited by Jerome Rothenberg,
University of California Press, 1968.

MUD, SKY, LITHOGRAPH

She stood blackened, not like ink or coal but like
the depth of the well.

Shining dark beneath the glisten of water,
she sang to the sparrows until they came to her.

She emerged from the shadows
with two arms extended, covered with crows.

Her eyes curved beneath the weight of long nights;
it took a thousand snow geese to lead her back to the surface.

The trees, one by one, bowed to her:
four-plated, etched, hand-colored.

Blue Heron, extending one leg,
invited her into the shadow-ripples of sun.

And she grasped at the moment, etched her fingernails into it,
as the planets spun beyond her fingertips—

She believed one vision could change everything:
it began with the wetlands recorded in relief, in lithograph, mixed ink.

The birds sang *Lullaby* in the breeze:
she painted Mamo goose on a canyon's red,

The wind and rain came to her then, speaking:
Turn and rise, Woman, with your red dance of cranes.

And she flew, wrapped green;
she flew, sun piercing her eye—

THE DAY

With water-sky and fire-hands,
we drag the sun,
a walrus, to the other side.
We pull, laughing and singing,
uvai, uvai, uvai.
The wind, our voices,
The wind, where we came from.
Our feet, wrapped in sealskin,
walk like bears
over the ice:
What's here today
will be different tomorrow,
the stars echoing the day,
aye, aye, yek.

IN YOUR BONES

He said, Bones.
He said, Bones, bones, bones, bones, rock.
(It echoed that way in me.)
And I said, Yes, yes (like water).
He said, with finality of ending summer,
Best thing that ever happened.
He spoke with the sounds of cranes in his throat.

His voice joins the voices flitting through me now like phantoms,
haunting, arousing . . .
It is night. The sun has moved much further north.
I close my eyes and try to sleep
but time has made creases in the sky
until it's impossible to see
the North Pole, the bending lights of God.

I hear my sister saying, Well, yeah, if you could do *that*
[listen to your soul]
then you'd have all the answers. Then it'd be easy.
I have not said to her, Yes that's why I do have all the answers. It *is* easy.
I do not want to argue.

I believe in voices. I believe in the traveling words of souls.
All I need are hours and quiet, shifting skies moving the sun and moon.
Even science craves the listening.
We have put satellites into space now.
We have telephones now in places
where there are no roads or running water.
We want to know they're real, the voices, our souls.

I type a number into my phone; the voice from my bones answers,
and suddenly everything, every place every person exist at once.
He says he just left a meeting to discuss the misuse of village *honey bucket*
     receptacles.

He laughs and says, It's like we're still living in the dark ages here huh?
I answer, No it's like you still have the light before the darkness.

WHALE HUNTING

If someone in the village is angry at you and not speaking, you may ride to the edge of the ice in spring and the whale hunting captains will be there with their crew, and aluminum boats pulled behind snow machines, walrus intestine waterproofing.

The wives and children will be coming and going with coffee and reindeer stew and you can shut down your snow-go and sit at the edge of the ice waving, sipping coffee, watching the water and pack ice float by steaming, and it is spring and the man whom you thought loved you is angry and not speaking.

The wife of the whaling captain serves the food; the crew informs you women are not allowed in hunting boats; bad luck; the oldest son climbs in the hunting skiff this year for the first time, and that son—who next year, on his 21st birthday, is murdered in Nome and dumped off the jetty—he shows you, *If you take this wooden oar and press the rounded end to your ear like this and the flat end into the sea*... You can stand bent over the edge, listening to the drifting songs of whales call from the depth of places you will never see.

TELL ME YOUR DAY

When you can't tell someone
about the berries on the hillside
and Venus whispering into the dawn,
the emptiness grows
like a cold, strong North wind
you must struggle against to get home—
If you cannot tell someone
about the long walk,
the rabid fox, the single shot,
the seal you brought home and skinned,
then what is left but darkness and sleep?
If you cannot tell
about the white-out conditions,
the reindeer on the mountain,
the ice fog moving like a polar bear at you,
then you become the blurred line of sky over ocean.
Tell me your day—
chopping wood, threading a needle,
gathering the small clams that wash up on the shore—

WATER

There are three kinds of water:
        hidden, frozen and gushing.
There are three kinds of being human:
        ice, water and snow.
There are three kinds of hearts,
and three kinds of Gods.

Have you ever heard the music of the Arctic ice
        each day shifting
frozen into a taut vibration, like strings
struck by wind,
a slow creaking of water hidden between?

When I love you,
I am water and rain,
and also that vast ice cap singing.
Can you forgive me
for the cold of winter storms
that wrap the moon with a gauze of sky-ice?
Can you forgive me
for the muddy melting slush of impassable spring?

Some waters emerge from the sand only in moonlight:
        it takes a certain patience.
There is consolation in the promise
that the water never leaves;
it is, instead, an assurance of transformation.

Water gives, and it takes.
It speaks to us only
if we listen.
Listen first,
and then I will love you, imperfectly,
with the erratic turning of seasons,
with the mystery of water seeping in
when we are not looking.

And then, in the piecing together and falling apart,
in the slow iceberg drift and the gentle drip, drip,
we can pardon each other
for the paths we have not taken.

Time Dilation

If you're traveling at 9/10ths the speed of light
things look shorter, and the faster you travel
the more you weigh until you become infinitely heavy.
If I leave Earth in a spaceship
and I'm traveling nearly 186,000 miles per second,
I can travel for one week into space
and another week back,
and 65 years have elapsed on Earth.
If I could travel the speed of light,
time would stand still—
I would reach infinity.

You cannot know it yet
but this is a love poem.
It is about the hours and miles
of a woman trying to reach a man
who has no idea
how much his every gentleness
erases time.

Please, stroke my hair.
Ask me, again, if I'm okay.
I want to believe in the speed of light.

It was the light that taught me about the speed of earth and travel
and love I couldn't imagine yet.
Me, still, just a normal body of mass
held to the Earth by gravity,
the hours shoving me forward with long, skinny arms—

It is possible to dilate time
or even stop it altogether.
Turn and walk east
until you get to the large rocks
and then climb to the top.

It is a fact.
Someone, traveling not in a spaceship
but in the rocket propelled pulse of heart,
prays, each second, for love.
Someone stands in the wind on a rock
and sees a mystical shine in the eyes of someone else.
And someone smiles.
Someone sits on top of a mountain,
strokes the back of someone else's hand.
And winter wraps itself like glittery infinity
around one moment of us, caught in light and second—

DORCAS

Acts Ch. 9. The name Dorcas *is a Greek translation of the Aramaic name*
Tabitha, *meaning "gazelle".*

And we name our daughters Dorcas
or Tabitha. We remember gazelles
gentle in their gliding over tall grasses.
We put our hands on woven cloths
and we bind one piece to another
with needle and thread.
Because our daughters are beautiful.
They sing to the moon.
And we protect them from lions and jackals
by teaching them quiet and hidden.

When Dorcas died, we
gathered up the robes she had been sewing.
We washed her body, cried tears onto her pale skin
preparing her for other worlds.
Dorcas, our beautiful gazelle, had dreamed herself too fast
and high over stars and bird nests.

We wove the soft cloth to wrap around her,
and then we left her.
Alone in a room with God, anything can happen.
In her death, Dorcas sang to the water
until the spirits heard her longing
and wanted her return, to finish her earth-water-song.
Dorcas was born and she died and then she lived again:
This is how some women have come to believe in impossible things.

Sometimes women sing to Death
and sometimes Death wakes up.
We name our daughters Dorcas or Tabitha,
for gazelles, not for saints or goddesses,
because we want life to be gentle
with tall lilies and gliding spirits.
We want to believe in miracles,
but even more we want to believe
our daughters are indestructible, and still soft and free as gazelles.

We name our daughters Dorcas or Tabitha
that they might, in outrunning death,
find themselves alone with God—
eyes open, a breath, and nothing more asked.

ACKNOWLEDGMENTS

Thank you to these publications, where the following poems previously appeared:

"Tower of Babel," *Malpais Review; Spring, 2012*

"Numbers," *North American Review, Vol. 296, #1; Winter, 2011*

"Mud, Sky, Lithograph," *Adobe Walls Anthology#2, 2010;*
Nominated for Pushcart Prize, 2011,

"The Day," *Rhino; 2007*

"In Your Bones," and "Whale Hunting," *Earthships A New Mecca Poetry Collection; 2007*

RICHARD BRODERICK

Attention is the highest form of prayer.

—*Simone Weil*

RICHARD BRODERICK

My writing is the distillation of a wandering mind anchored by an attentive spirit. I have been blessed with two children, a son and a daughter, both of whom I love fiercely. I've told them many times that, though I hope they enjoy a measure of worldly success and a happy life, my ultimate ambition as their father is that they possess two things: a big heart and a deep spirit.

I like to think that a big heart and a deep spirit constitute the region from which my poetry originates as well the qualities that characterize it at its best. It pleases me if upon occasion a poem of mine moves or amuses listeners but I am never embarrassed if it fails to do so as long it fails on the terms I have laid out for myself.

If civilizations can be said to possess souls, then the seat of our collective soul in the Western world is the will. Logically, as Jung said, the opposite of love is hatred, but psychologically the opposite of love is the will to power. Where the drive to control exists, he said, there can be no love. And where love exists, there can be no drive to control. To me, imagination is an expression of love, of the abandonment of control. This is so even if, in the end, the products of imagination must have comprehensible structure if they are to communicate with others rather than be nothing more than an autistic outburst of impenetrable self-reference.

In our part of the globe, we regularly confuse fantasy, the willful imposition of our wish-dreams upon reality, with imagination, the willingness to let go of the will and to allow reality to enter into us from all sides and from there, if we are lucky, take shape as sounds, images, movement and ideas. The craft of poetry is not the ability to will poems into existence; it is the gift of being able to write well under inspiration – to be ready, pen in hand, when the muse descends.

Poetry, like all genuine expressions of the imagination, is a product of what Keats called Negative Capability: i.e., the capability (and willingness) to live in doubt, confusion and anxiety without an irritable grasping after certainty. As I sometimes tell people who come to me for guidance in writing poetry, judgment is the death of the imagination. In the absence of imagination there can be no poetry just as there can be no music, dance, art and theater – or, for that matter, love and compassion, themselves the products of our ability to image our own humanity and the humanity of others. To open ourselves to poetry is to heed the invitation still offered to us even today, when the call is often drowned out by the getting and spending of contemporary "culture" – the invitation to connect with our deepest selves and, in doing so, join the never-exhausted banquet of solidarity with our fellow beings.

—Richard Broderick

Listening to a CD of Glenn Gould Performing "The Goldberg Variations"

You can hear him in the background
if you listen closely, his voice a little hoarse
and off-key, creating its own counterpoint.
Faint at first, the crackling sound builds
as his fingers dig deep into the score,
swelling in the slower movements, fading
in the fast, though never disappearing.
Strange he felt compelled to add
his own wordless singing to the track,
even if it meant marring the perfection
of his performance, or maybe *because*
it meant marring that perfection,
as if over the years every time he sat down
at a keyboard he found it harder and harder
not to notice how much a grand piano resembles
a coffin, the lid propped open to reveal
steel tendons and felt-covered knucklebones.
And so he sang, and still sings, heartfelt
if out of tune, his spirit living on in the spaces
between the notes, where we all live,
stepping lightly up and down the staff,
leaping nervously over every pause, never
more than one full-stop away from silence.

All Present And Accounted For

Earth is the heaven of animals.
It is only on earth they are fully
present and no where else. (Even
in your dreams, the wolf and
the snake are no more than shadows
of your projection.) No brown bear

ever waded the fall run, catching
salmon, but wishing he were
someplace else. No milk cow
plans for the future or dreams
of changing places with the sleek
Jersey on the cover of this month's

Dairy Digest. Dogs do not fall
into a brown study, cats have
no second thoughts, the honey-
bee gives it full attention
to the hive or the flower.
Horse and cattle may be driven

to distraction by biting flies
(themselves a model of insistent
presence), but in doing so they
give themselves to madness
without stint. That goat you saw
while out driving in the country

wasn't really sullen; that was some
feeling of your own you'd rather
leave behind standing on a hillside
glaring at the road. Yes,
you have seen apes and lions
looking bored, but that was

at the zoo, where they were trapped
in man-made enclosures, boxes
like the ones you've always lived in.
So maybe the soul – the soul you're
not sure animals even possess –
maybe that's the name you give

to the part of yourself you have
no power to withhold. And maybe
heaven, maybe that's where you
hope someday to be fully present,
the garden where we'll all be
reborn into our animal selves

Autumn Tutorial

Summer's over.
The trees shed their leaves.
The days grow brighter
even as they get shorter;
so much sky was hidden
behind that shade!
Is this how you want me
to come to you, Lord —
self-disarmed, a broken
pane of glass where
light and air both stream?
Is that why I've noticed
the less I speak the more
you seem inclined to listen?

NIGHT SHIFT

Tonight your father returns to you as a woman,
death freeing him to face in two directions.
It's awkward for a little while:

his bony frame draped in crinoline,
his mouth shining beneath lip gloss, the long
silence he's endured making his voice rough,

pitched somewhere in the middle range,
like an old-fashioned clock on the verge of striking.
Now you can see the softness that was there all along

even before he yielded to illness, in the maternal impulse
behind the years you've spent nurturing his memory.
If he picks you up bodily now as he use to

when you were a little boy, don't turn away.
Don't resist. Let him plant a fatherly kiss.
It's not just your dream anymore. It's also his.

COTE DE VALAIS

after Rilke's French poems

Take heed of how these mountain freshets,
spilling into the stone-dressed drains
that bear them through the village,
go on making their own weather,
thick clouds here, a deep blue sky elsewhere,
waking each rock they touch, turning
every obstacle into a fountain of song.
And if a small current happens to wander
into a side-channel, her sisters
come quickly to take her by the hand
and send her tumbling again downhill,
crying out, 'Hurry along now! There are
flowerbeds thirsting in the valley!
Young brides waiting to be quickened
by a shower of pearls!'

EVERY RIVER

A meadow gone soggy underfoot.
Crops damaged by a hailstorm.
A desert in bloom.
A child swept away by the current.

Every river is a reminder
of cause-and-effect,
a record of what happened
at a distance,
in the past,
somewhere out of sight.

Whose heart has thawed.

Whose heart remains
locked in winter.

BETWEEN THE COVERS

The books I left out in the backyard last night
are swollen this morning with dew,
loaves of raw dough leavened by starlight,
the lungs of asthmatic children
breathing deeply at summer camp.
The fresh air has done them good.
Calmed by contact with nature,
they speak more slowly now,
the interval between their words
a little longer than before.

I pick them up and bring them inside.
They have witnessed how the moon
starves herself each month
in a nervous bid for attention.
They know by the thoughtful way I turn them over
and run my fingers across their pages
that they are valued for their inner worth,
for their depth and even their flaws,
like a beloved wife grown
fat and beautiful over the years.

Song of the Fat Woman Swimming off Cocoa Beach

I come here every chance I get.
The ocean always wants me,
always takes me in its arms.

When it lifts me, I grow buoyant.
My edges dissolve with each salt lick.

Now I'm a first-time mother again,
lulling my newborn to sleep
to the sound of the waves,

now a teenager sunbathing
with my friends,

now a chubby toddler,
wading naked in the surf,
too caught up in play
to hear my own mother calling me:

"Come away from the water now!
It's time to eat!"

Boys Fishing

All the way across the pond
I hear them curse their tackle,
their tangled reels,
watch as they snag lures
in low-hanging branches,
while below, their
blurred reflections
rock calmly on the surface.

Who are these quiet spirits
rising to join them after
a long swim in the depths?
Sitting on the grass,
I glimpse my own reflection,
finding no name for estrangement,
no memory of when
my edgy shore-bound "I"
divided from the "me"
swimming peacefully
in motherly brown water.

Having freed his line,
one of the boys casts
across his own image,
calls to his friend and cackles.
I watch as he cranks
and cranks the reel,
trying to tow his
own shadow back to land.

Swimming Laps

I swim an hour as if to chase the boy
I was, drowning, drowned,

beneath the closing waters
of the past, the boy who splashed

all day down by the beach, who could
hold his breath until his father,

watching, reached the point of panic.
Now, breathless, my father lies

at depths beyond the gasp of fear,
while in the pool, just past a mile

earned lap by lap, I seem to slip
inside another skin in which

the boy I was and the man I am
swim toward each other, breathing

easy now, side-by-side, afloat
in memory, our native element.

August Sunset from the Highest Point in St. Paul

How we'd like to hope that our lives, too,
will turn to gold just before they set,
the all-too-familiar silhouette of the city
backlit, burnished, with a refulgent glow
beneath a slowly-developing, redemptive
vision of the earth's rim lifting to meet
a sky flushed with rose-colored flame,
and then, as darkness finally settles in,
lights coming on in the river valley far below.

THE BOXING LESSON

"Keep it light, boys. Keep it light,
"my father would shout from the sidelines,
meaning light on our feet, dancing and circling,
never coming in direct at your opponent,
like that time my youngest brother
walked right into my straight-armed left
and knocked himself flat.

It was as if his sons were figures
in a myth whose feet might take root
the instant we stopped moving,
a suit of chainmail bark creeping up
over our thighs and trunks, freezing
us in place so we'd end up reeling
punch drunk before the fists of any breeze.

If, as he taught us, I look for movement
out of the corner of my eye
("The punch you don't see coming
is the one you've got to watch for"),
I can glimpse him out there in the blue arena,
dancing and circling, always moving,
as he boxes Death himself,
snapping back the hooded head
with a crisp one-two.

Upon Receiving My Brother's Ashes

Good-bye, brother. And hello. Our childhood
died with you in that sealed Florida room
where you exiled yourself, the shades
drawn, your swollen heart burst at last,
nothing in the refrigerator, the TV on.
Now there's no one to ask
the name of the neighbor boy's cousin
who fell through the ice on Mirror Lake
and drowned, or of the candy store
out on the highway, or where we were the day
we drank homemade root beer, then played
pirate ship with other kids in a dusty barn.
All I have of you now is this bronze box
filled with ashes (not even a proper urn),
the sweepings of your life. What would I
find if I pried open its seal and peeked inside?
Some powdery substance, gritty and fine,
like the beach we used to play on, the sand
so hot in the mid-day sun that even
in the time it took us to run to the lake
the soles of our feet would burn.

ON THE HIGHWAY TO HEAVEN

Out here, fiery wrecks
are restored,
overturned LP tanker trucks
blaze with a flame that
burns but does not consume,

the twisted hulks of loaded
station wagons
carrying families
to the vacations they will never
return from are righted,
back in lane,

father behind the wheel
permanently stalled
in that happy moment
just before the crash
when his eye was caught
by his son pointing out
the hawk forever lifting off
from a fencepost.

And here the sleepy travelers
wake in time,
this time,
to pull their cars back
across the center line

and drunks
crawl out from smoking heaps,
grin crookedly and ask
for another drink,

and all the girls who ever
disappeared
hitchhiking home from college
stand beside the road,
resurrected in their youth,
innocent thumbs

stuck out again.

JESUS OF WALMART

They liked the radiant smile, his upbeat manner
and so, despite a scanty work record –
"Assistant carpenter, then three years
wandering the hills" -- they hired him
as a greeter, the wages from his full-time,
28-hour-a-week job not enough to cover
the company's health insurance. "Get sick
around here and you just have to heal yourself,"
muttered a disgruntled "associate," a 50-ish mother
whose crippled daughter got up the very
next day and walked, everybody calling it
a miracle, just like that special order
of tee-shirts that sold for $1.99 each.
Now he wanders the aisles in a pair
of plastic sandals made in China,
reminding shoppers of special savings
they'll find if they only keep on searching,
pointing out the counter where
you can redeem coupons clipped from
somebody's discarded newspaper,
consoling the single moms when they
discover food-stamps can't be used
to buy the sugary cereal their fatherless
kids clamor for each morning. In aisles
lined with desolate frowns he smiles,
asking weary late-night shoppers if he
can help, talking softly, respectfully
to those who have never known anything
but contempt and the presumption

of guilt. To the illegals sneaking in
after a hard day of underpaid work,
men named Jose, woman called Maria,
he speaks in tongues they haven't heard
since leaving home in search of plenty.
The lonely, the desperate, the stoned,
those who've given up hope, he steers
ever-so-gently away from Hardware
with its brackets of nails and coils
of rope. Look at me, he says.
I have no home, no place to rest
my head. But even on a Saturday night
when it's raining outside, and the last
bus left 15 minutes ago, there is a place
that's always open, offering light,
offering the chance that when the price
of going on even another day seems
beyond reach, you'll find what you need
and it will cost you little, it will cost you
nothing. Just heed my words,
he urges everyone. Have a little faith.

The Long Drive Down

The horizon's still out there,
still crouching low,
still circling like a pack
of proverbial wolves.
It knows that no matter
how many miles I drive
today or tomorrow,
I'll never catch up,
and when I finally do,
it'll swallow me whole.
In the late afternoon light,
it looks hazy and indistinct,
like my recollection of what
I had for lunch yesterday
or who I met with afterward.
Not at all sharp and clear
like the memory of the words
my father said to me just before
he died or what he and I
were wearing at that moment
or the way his hands
quivered like warm air
shimmering above a long
stretch of open highway
or how he kept gazing
into the distance as if
he were watching something
only he could see, something
that had always been far away
but now was growing near.

Dichos

based upon dichos – "sayings"— *posted*
on many Latin American vehicles,
especially trucks and buses.

1.

You need an open heart
to have an open mind.
Not everything gold glitters.
A cactus wears all those spines
to protect sweet flesh inside.

Every time you come near, I realize –
I don't need wings to fly!
Close your eyes now.
Look at yourself.

See how beautiful?

2.

I need to leave home
but don't know
if I'll be able
to find my way home again.
I need to flee now
but can't find
the bent key that
opens the broken lock.

We've filled so many cups
with our tears,
we could supply
our own salt flats.

At this time of day,
the high bridge is only visible
above the treeline.
I see wild geese flying away
and I understand why,

but don't know how.

3.

I went to bed empty
but woke up full of you.

It keeps happening
over and over no matter
how many hours
I spend each day
baling out and patching up
my brain's leaky hull.
How can I even call them
"my dreams"
when every dream I have
has only one real star
and that star's real name
is really you?

I close my eyes.
I drift off to sleep,
but it just turns out
to be the nightly lull
before the curtain goes up
and the show begins.
Once more, I'm sure
you'll be pleased to know,
I went to bed empty

but woke up full of you.

4.

Never give a ride to a witch.
When the snakes start gossiping,
it's because the mule has died.
Look — now you've lost the shortcut.

No one will cry for you
just for the sake of crying.
Go ahead and suffer because of love;
there is no salvation for the envious.
Jealousy is the only revenge.

You want my advice?
Four words only —

I will remember you.

Dark Day

Dark day that doesn't brighten past dawn,
all your hours are waking hours.
I love your soft breath, your quiet voice,
your palate of subdued colors.
Teach me the spirit of watchful waiting.
Rouse my every moment from its sleep.

ACKNOWLEDGMENTS

The following poems have previously appeared in these publications

Journals

Atlanta Review: "Swimming Laps," "August Sunset from the Highest Point in St. Paul"

Eclipse: "Between the Covers,"

Lief: "Dichos 1., 4.

North Dakota Quarterly: "On the Highway to Heaven"

Poetry East: "Autumn Tutorial," "Cote de Valais," "Every River," "The Long Drive Down," "Boys Fishing," "Upon Receiving My Brother's Ashes," "Dark Day"

Rhino: "Night Shift"

Slant: "All Present and Accounted For"

Turtle Quarterly: "Listening to a CD of Glenn Gould Performing 'The Goldberg Variations'"

Anthologies

"The Boxing Lesson," *Perfect in Their Art: Poems about Boxing*, University of Southern Illinois Press, (2003)

KATHERINE DIBELLA SELUJA

Where there was a life, now there is form...And the form spoken breathes something of that life out into the world again. It restores a human presence; hidden in the lines....and so the result is a permanent intimacy;...

—Mark Doty

KATHERINE DiBELLA SELUJA

Jim was dying of renal failure. The older nurses called me into Jim's room to check his blood pressure. They knew that as a nursing student I had most likely never seen the pounding pulse of 250/175 that is consistent with end stage kidney disease. Years of overly sweetened blood coursing through his kidneys had weakened the delicate maze of glomerular filters. Sharp edged glucose crystals had poked holes in every twisting calculi. His salted crystalline skin, his yellowed eyes, his distended abdomen mounding under the bed sheet were all symptoms I was instructed to observe. What I noticed was the stillness in his room. Late July sunlight slanted through the window in an undisturbed manner. Only essential functions were ordered for Jim, so his room was absent of the usual hospital bustle. In the afternoons, while the nurses were finishing their charting, I would sit with Jim. The 2 p.m. quiet filled his room and we would talk.

About nothing I can particularly recall. No potent life advice, no acute perspective from a man so near the grave. What I remember is the stillness. The peace that comes from knowing you are almost done. No more schedule, no more blood tests, no more updating your CV. And it is into this calm that I venture when I write. It is this stillness that I invoke and work towards, whatever the subject. A newborn's illness, a family loss, a moment in the summer garden. I ask Jim's peace to guide me.

Most health care workers recognize that they carry their patients' stories with them and are often deeply affected by these stories. The nature of nursing, particularly when caring for critically ill individuals, is one of rapid intimacy. We are all required to reveal much more of ourselves during serious illness than we normally would in our daily lives. After many years in healthcare, I realized my cupboard was getting pretty full. I needed to find a way to honor, respect and release some of these stories. Mark Doty speaks of this honoring and intimacy in his essay, "Still Life with Oysters and Lemon":

> Where there was a person, a voice, a range and welter of experience...now there are only lines and images. Where there was a life, now there is form...And the form spoken breathes something of that life out into the world again. It restores a human presence; hidden in the lines....and so the result is a permanent intimacy; we are brought into relation with the perceptual character, the speaking voice, of someone we probably never knew, someone no one can know now, except in this way. (pg 50)

This "permanent intimacy" is a propelling force in my writing. I have been inspired by poets such as Dorianne Laux and Marie Howe. I prefer the stark contrast of placing intense life events into poetic and lyrical form. Poetry and short prose are my vehicles for releasing and honoring many of my patients' stories. I will usually start with one of the stories that has been living within me, sometimes for much longer than I may even realize.

The seed for a piece may be an image, a name, a diagnosis, a set of symptoms or a certain smell (hospital hallways in early summer). Then I let that guiding thought unravel. If I'm doing my job and paying attention, I will arrive somewhere unexpected, land in the midst of the deeper significance of that image or sound or memory. I was recently asked if I felt I was somehow invading a patient's privacy by writing about them. When a patient's life events and our time together impact me or imprint me with that sense of permanent intimacy and I am prompted to write, I see no infringement of privacy. I see only reverence.

There is a growing body of information that speaks to the healing value of writing for individuals experiencing all types of stress, illness or trauma. Caregivers will frequently have their own secondary responses to their patients' stories. We all share a deep longing to ground, to connect, to make sense of life events that are seemingly random and often traumatic. I am responding to this longing here, within these pages. The mining of my patients' stories, and my responses to them, is a deeply fulfilling and satisfying work.

Included here are 11 pieces from *No Storm Like Him*, the manuscript dedicated to my schizophrenic alcoholic brother. There are three primary voices within the manuscript, that of the psychotic brother, the sister and another authoritative/narrative voice. These pieces reveal the fear, the chaos, the confusion of living with mental illness. They are speaking for the individual experiencing the illness, as well as the family members who must also walk that road. They are attempting to "open the locked ward door" and bring light to the mystery and stigma that is often associated with mental illness. I am particularly dedicated to this subject and welcome comments and community around the feelings and ideas expressed within these pieces.

—Katherine DiBella Seluja

Ref: Doty, Mark *Still Life with Oysters and Lemon*, Beacon Press, 2001.

BLUE VASE

empty

translucent container

to hold your only duty

how many bouquets did you miss

when I gaze through blue glass

thorns come into view

long stemmed wonder

garland of barren questions

and what of the funneled calla

the wilting lily

baby's breath

torn and frayed

still your tangled roots

mildew in grey water

rest now   floating

brown leaf posy

DEHISCENCE

Questions fell
down from the trees

the summer my sister lay in bed

each one a delicate boomerang
a pair of pale green wings

Lucent sap thick on our thumbs
as children we split them wide

pressed thin blades to noses and chins
flaunting sudden protuberances

A pod had taken root in her belly
and unfurling its haughty head

hissed capricious commands
to her indentured being

I was a seed with pale wings
spinning on wanton wind

falling to gravel or pavement
questing for moisture below

On the ground, the wing serves little purpose

Smoldering
in an August of no answers

my family daily swept the walk
hoarding dried piles of query

barter for respite or rain

You will find it in the stillness

You will christen him with saline
wash the noise and tape away

acetone ghosting from the room

you will wrap his tiny form
in the sheet they call morgue pack

only pale white morning moons remain

when ventilator's incessant
waves of breathing come to rest

when persistent pulsing
monitor is done

when the shining beads of moisture
inside his breathing tube are gone

pale white morning moons remain

It is then that you will feel
the ancient mantle

on your chest
drop like sodden wool

yet light as infant's breath

it is then that you will bow
you head and mumble ragged prayer

silent   awkward   praise

WHEN I THINK OF BIRTH

When I think of birth a burning pressure
the summer her rabbit died

she prayed every day to the virgin
pleading for a sister this time

When I think of birth heat unfolding
tiny green leaves on a stem

tight fisted blue toed wailing
weight to fill a dresser drawer

All my grandmothers babies
(she said it was really so)
spent several weeks in the bureau

Think of birth unwinding
a newborn to fit in your hand

skin barely translucent
arms flung out to the dawn

When I find a birth and a story
a woman carries her worries alone

each week that belly swelling
making its push toward the earth

My mother was born after midnight
midwife at my grandmothers side

cold linguine and sauce on the table
counting the seconds till light

Think of birth and a barrel
rolling your rain down the hill

Vena Cava Fable

Their baby was born with a backwards heart
aorta snarled in vena cava

and that heart would gurgle and drain

the mother   adored the crystal powder
sparked with a bluish hue

that mother would snuffle and wheeze

the father   bench pressed three hundred fifty
arm inked with a heart of thorns

that muscle would pump and flex

They became accustomed to
pull and flail of baby thin ribs

swollen membranes
a penlight could shine right through

or a searchlight held high from police cruiser
flooding years of hustle and street

and the baby becoming more blue

They called in the fingertip surgeon
delicate hands to rotate a heart

that surgeon would scrub and glisten
glisten right down to the bone

that baby chest was his altar
sutured with reconciliation

and this offering to donate my heart

UPON HEARING THAT AN URUGUAYAN MOTHER
FED HER CHILDREN GRASS

May you never cook leaves and salt
and offer it to hungry faces

yerba and oil sit alone on the shelf
never cook leaves and salt

May you never carry your baby
down Ramon Anador begging for milk or rice

knocking at thresholds trembling
never carry your baby down

May you never long for two
stomachs   one to ruminate cud

one a chamber for holding
both contract when empty

May you never forage the yard
dried *butiá* wrinkled and brown

soaking to soften the veins
pounding to break down the fiber

weighing each boney piece
never cook leaves and salt

SANTUARIO

What then denied to us hath heaven on man bestowed?
Queen Penthesilea, Battle of Troy

I walk the fifteen miles   narrow road
dip my hands into Chimayó

grains of holy dirt on my tongue
invoke St. Agatha   the Amazons

women of iridescent scars

at the shrine of the Virgin
write my name in willow leaves

and when the moon is full again
after the emesis and the drains

after stitches tread across my chest
Penitentes bearing their crosses

after the surgeon says   you'll have to be vigilant
your results are black velvet strewn with sand

no more postponement or delay
I will paint in the river at night   sketch in all of my margins

call to the shining ravens breeching near the bosque

at the altar filled with tissue paper blessings
in the chapel draped with infant shoes and crosses

I pray to those fierce archers
breasts sacrificed for the sake of the bow

YOU IN 'BURQUE

Waves of love
undulate La Bajada
inflate two man rafts on Cochiti Lake
flow through Santo Domingo Crafts Fair   fill
hand coiled pots and shoes of weary toddlers
sticky with honey and fry bread
fingerprints on the dashboard love
arroyo overflowing
pebbles and sand love
spin the wind sock
slippery when wet crosswinds love
light the night sky
San Felipe casino road sign love   my heart
playing for you Tuesdays and Thursdays through August
the all heart reunion tour
stopping at Pueblo Gas not because it's cheaper
but because it fills itself   runs
on its own combustion   love's spark plugs
set with perfect timing
no caution shoulder work love   no
Bernalillo Gypsum factory love
Balloon Fiesta hot air love
mile marker 263 love
scaling the Marriott Pyramid like some love crazed
traveler with a view good enough to see me in La 'Fe
you in 'Burque

Even though your dorm faces the Sandias,
they named the building Jemez

THESE WORDS FOR MY DAUGHTERS

Sing with the ravens whenever they call

let the youngest and eldest go first
know the secret to your grandmother's sauce

even when the moon is new
be fearless with I'm sorry

watch for beauty in a stone, your world in a sparrow egg
never say no to a sting ray gliding the Gulf

refuse to live without song
say yes to the hummingbird moth that hovers

at the edge   keep the dates of the solstice
forget the day your heart cracked

wild fescue grows from the fissures
share even when you think you have nothing

one serving goes further than you know
pull off the gloves and build

your life with bare hands

No Storm Like Him

One thin crack
in the plastic sign

on the locked ward door
winds its way through

Authorized Personnel Only
like a branch

of the Hackensack River
where we used to play

dried mud thick
on our shoes split

in so many places
our mother's face

when she said *We just readmitted your brother.*
He told us his crystals were melting.

Waiting for the orderly
to turn his key

I turn back

to our winter childhood
clubhouse under the cellar stairs

wooden clipboard
blue graph paper

we were base camp
guardians of snow

charted drift
and temperature

graphed hope
for Sunday night storms.

One day I found him frozen
in the kitchen

crushed words stuck to his tongue

psychosis   schizoid   mania

what was this illness of ice?

Now grey clouds
and thorazine doses increase

he wanders the blizzard alone
no guide rope tied to the door

unique as each stellar dendrite
no two of him alike.

YOU WOULD HAVE TO BE ADIRONDACK GREEN MOUNTAINS

to know why the brother
who climbed in through dark windows

was sent there
farm school in the hills

what seemed like reward to a Laura Ingalls girl
was something more like exile

You would have to be A-frame construction
fifteen foot beams

hold the weight of February
walk the last mile in

to sustain refuge rather than removal

You would long to be backseat quiet
past Albany grey granite
winding Glens Falls

to arrive at banishment, not retreat

You would dream the tacit bull
led through barnyard gate
shot with nervous fingers and a .22

to know anything more than slaughter

PANTOUM FOR GREYSTONE LOCKED WARD

There are men who are old and writhing
a nurse who never slows down her pace
trembling hands their prayers are a tithing
mumbled words on their lips have no taste

A nurse who never slows down her pace
in that warren of wards I find you
wax eyes in a motionless face
thorazine doses that blind you

In that warren of wards I find you
face dull as the wax on the floor
judge's court order that binds you
wired glass double locks on the door

Words dull as the wax on the floor
feet that shuffle and shake
wired glass double locks on the door
low howl only sound you can make

Feet that shuffle and rake
slow tear drools from your eye
soft growl only sound you can make
cracked window broken slice of the sky

Slow fear slips from my eye
cotton wrapped tight round your wrist
cracked window small slice of the sky
walls that have never been kissed

Cotton wrapped tight round your wrist
stigmata bright and binding
walls that have never been kissed
there are men who are old and writhing

TELEPHONE, 4 A.M.

Wrapped in dark muslin night

sharp scream of ringing phone
his stumbling voice   gagging

emergency room   again

and you think
what if there were a box to keep him in

somewhere to store him away

to bring out with rainy weather
can't go to the lake today

when each white square has its penciled letter
every puzzle piece its mate

then you would have time to listen

unravel every line
you'd be awake already

scooping vanilla chip ice cream
your favorite blue porcelain bowl

the one with the crack that resembles
shining scar on his forehead

how sharp that metal gutter
the night he flew from the roof

SPINNING WITH THORAZINE
with excerpts from *The Joy of Hand Spinning* website

Charge the carder
by taking it in your left hand

   Now he's a pillow or a block of ice

with your right hand lay staples
of wool across the metal pins

   wrapped in cotton gauze
   eyes a matted quilt

   lashes pulled mid-stitch

distribute the wool evenly
over the entire card

   soft thump of cotton slippers
   gathering lint from the floor

until card teeth are barely showing

   young woman in the dayroom corner
   pulls at wisps of air

what hospice nurses call

   reaching for the angels

YOU WERE PICTURING A '68 MUSTANG

A watercolor landscape propped against a tree
orchard sunlight blurs into painted sunlight

and you want to step inside
the hood vent   square cut   spokes on the wheel

The psychiatrist said *It's all in the bloodlines*

> *We can trace the illness back 3 to 400 hundred years*
> *eye folds   nail ridges   slacking skin*

You only want to be part of the tour
see the form on the page

the slanting brush   the upstroke   spool of light

> The shrink jumps in the car
> complaining about backseat drivers then

> tells you to take
> a left at the light

> *It's all a matter of proteins, we'll have it cracked*
> *in 3 or 4 years*

And you
go along for the ride

switching directional signals   alternating your speed
searching the rearview mirror

Images much closer than they seem

Delirium tremens

Let the glass sweat and bleed
   let the foam run dry

walk away from the drink
   and let the shaking begin

turn to the buzzing in your head
   flies at an oozing wound

canyons scream at your feet
   tear down

Budweiser poster throw away
   Michelob key   hold tight

to that wad of sheets heaving
   at the edge of your bed

vessel of your salvation that you despise
   your bed is a boat and its swaying

   swinging to a reggae beat
a beat that soothes and sickens

   and the ants just won't stop crawling
treading down your arm

a track for the beetles to follow
last night you must have killed 20

snapping crack of blue green carapace
    beneath your trembling feet

Conversing with Cirrhosis

You should be glad it never happened. No drunken sperm of yours flailing its tail sideways could have ever found her lopsided egg. Yes, she was your childhood sweet heart and yes, her family moved to the block just as June was beginning to thrum, her younger sister running hide and seek with the fireflies and rugged limbs of oak. But back to you and your soaring liver enzymes, climbing higher than the tree in their side yard. If you had borne an infant together, would its skin have gone as yellow as the edges of your eyes are now? Would it have screamed at night, its belly sucking in all the air in the room? Just as your belly is filling now with fluid, peritoneal fluid, squeezing backwards out of the wrinkled straw that was your portal vein, your liver a dishpan sponge floating in the morning sink.

But we were discussing babies—or one that wasn't and how you can still see it's chestnut eyes gleaming in the dark, feel it's fingers clutching at your chest, as you stroke your protruding abdomen and marvel how after all these years and so many Sloe Gin Fizzes, a man like you could somehow, finally, gestate.

NEWS OF A BROTHER'S DEATH

Don't kid yourself
it's nothing like a movie
no subtitles to clarify meaning
no forewarning minor key
no change of lens to soften
the edges of scene

only my clinic office
a patient's nebulizer hum
nurses calling pressures from another room
rude light from cubicle window
glare of black corded phone
and that sudden break in the real
right after I hear Tom say
the police found him   in his apartment   on the floor

OF CALAMINE AND HONEY

Make a list
of all that is broken

sparrow egg
his cherry tree face

and all that is amniotic

children's feet scuffle
over cracks in sidewalk

wide enough
for 3 small pebbles

and nests of wasp

you can't go on that way
only thorns to catch your fall

and his words
buzzing at your ankles

searching for the tender spot

ACKNOWLEDGMENTS

These pieces previously published in:

"Dehiscence," *Santa Fe Literature Review*, 2010

"You will find it in the stillness," *Adobe Walls*, 2010

"No Storm Like Him" and "News of a brother's death," *Touch: A Journal of Healing*, 2013; with "Of calamine and honey" and "Telephone, 4 a.m." forthcoming in the Fall of the same journal.

AARON A. ABEYTA

I love all the things there are,
and of all the fires
love is the only inexhaustible one

—Pablo Neruda

AARON A. ABEYTA

Dear Stewart, I must apologize for the delay in getting this to you. The truth of the matter is that I have struggled with this introduction for sometime now. Your instructions were clear, let the reader know what you were thinking and give them a bit of who you are as a writer, standard policy type stuff. After all, they are love poems, plain and simple, one of the old literary standbys, love, immortality, and God.

An introduction to such poems should be along the lines of *I see in my wife and love of my life, the hand of the world at work, and in that work, even the invisible and unnoticed gestures of her daily tasks, there is something the heart cannot define but feels it must.* This would be true of the poems I have sent you, and I hope in the way that writers hope that some reader will find that same gesture in their heart, and in so doing love their wife, lover or friend in a way that is complete.

There is, however, another truth in the poems, one that is more selfish, more dark perhaps. My last two books were the work of grief, the grief of loss and a despair that is like a hail storm to the abundant head of ripening grain. I will not get into the particulars of that here; those losses are well documented and there are stone monuments and dates to their time here on earth. The poems were intended to rescue me, self-rescue by the only survival skill I know to be effective, the saving word. I wondered if this admission, the forced march towards healing that these poems represent might put the readers off. Who among us, after all, prefers salt in their coffee?

So I began one day like all seekers must, I suppose, by looking for the brief kiss of God, love and hope in the things where only a poet might look. These poems began with the hypothesis of another author who claimed that the balance of two people meeting and therefore changing the world rested upon something as inconsequential as making it to a store on time so that the character in the story might purchase leg cream. I believed that assertion was so sad, and I was tired of being sad. Tired of the fallen buildings of my hometown, tired of the walls punctuated by the despair and anger of spray paint, tired of the shirtless drunk of main street whose mother was cruel and whose time in the foster care system was cruel too, tired of my own sadness and the poems such sadness breeds. I was tired and therefore chose not to rest, but to look for a way that love might be found, even if the leg cream was not purchased and the two lovers did not meet as was prescribed by science and the theories which have come to govern our world and the delicate spider web balance of time.

Later, I looked for the same gesture of love in other unorthodox and obscure places, a calculus problem, a topo map, a table with one leg shorter than the others, in the dawn release of a trout, in a sestina about El Paso, a villanelle about hummingbirds, wherever there might be the slightest grace and whisper of love, I looked, and it is my hope that with some of these poems I can help the reader find a similar place that is safe and touched by some brief yet lasting healing.

I will not presume that I have been saved or even healed, though I do feel better, and the fact that these poems will finally see the white light of the page helps in that process of healing and finding oneself in a better place.

You see Stewart, that is the power of the poem, it builds from silence, requires it even, but it is the poem which has always been made to sing. Somewhere between those two poles is where we all live, between the silence and the song there is our life, and it is the poem that mends and sews the two poles into a single understanding, a place where we love, and by love I mean living.

Much Peace,
a.

THE FRAGILE VESSEL

this fragile vessel is four hummingbirds
darting   hovering   tasting at lilacs
like bees   they seem to have only one purpose

to find what is sweet or beautiful   to linger
at the colorful mouths of returning spring
the fragile vessel that is four hummingbirds

has wings that cannot be seen
my body that is also four hummingbirds
like bees seems to have just one purpose

this particular human heart beats 132,480 times a day
opening and closing   it must beat for someone
this fragile vessel is four hummingbirds

tracing the flower's petals to where
the nectar sweet neck bows to the ground
i   like bees with a single purpose

hover at the scent of your spring neck
taste at the flower of your lilac eyes
like bees this particular heart has one purpose
a fragile vessel   this heart   four hummingbirds

LOVE POEM AFTER A PASSING ANTELOPE

i have come
to one of the old campaderos
there is this voice
that sounds like a breeze
and a red earth
impossibly clinging
to the last hours before dusk

from where i stand
in the dark circle
of a long ago removed corral
there is nothing but east ahead of me
and some faint image
a mirage of five antelope
not really running
but gliding windlike
over the sage and volcanic rock

there is something blind inside of me
like a love poem
some pit of the stomach uneasiness
that is almost beautiful
i cannot imagine
this place more clearly
than it is painted here today
clouds their bodies full of rain
resting their tiredness
on the sangre de cristos

114   aaron a. abeyta

something out here
on this loma
is trying to remember me
my scent downwind
in some cautious place
that only moves a few steps at a time
then grazes grazes
looks up and cannot remember

today out in the hills
that beg for rain
beneath the passing river noise
of a jet unzipping
the blue and gray sky
i am almost
face to face with you now
this singing wind
a Whitman soul that sends out
"filament filament filament"
you are thin legged   cautious
winter has treated you well
can i call you love
like a memory of grazing sheep
or are you something else
beautiful and singular
like a smile

i love you silent saturday
and something yes something
very old and repetitive loves me too
more gently than the earth
loves rain

more spiritually than a solitary tree
loves wind
more slowly than the moon
loves clouds
you passing thing
like 8 a.m. on a wednesday
the last of your voice
i love you
like something green and windy
in the first days of spring

A TRUE LOVE POEM

i meet him at dusk
in the field with the old
broken wagon
an ice hauler
from a river now
thinly frozen

this wagon
wheels missing
floor boards of missing teeth
my abuelito's
simple memory
of Orlando and his leaving
do you remember how he cried when he had to go

from here i can see
la otra vanda
the river stripped sticks
used to leap over fences
the herd Orlando and my
father followed
how it ended in autumn
and how one of the boys cried

my abuelito
says that sometimes
he feels like his old wagon
the loads the two of them
must've carried

their weight of ice
summers that melted
around them

here is your true love poem
Marcos Sanchez
it is an old man's words
from a wheelchair
the way his eyes
filled with thin tears
that did not fall
the way he
remembered Orlando
and only this boy heard

BROWN INCA BESIDE A RIVER

because i love you
random things come into my head
i will   apparently for no reason   and sometimes out loud
think things like urubamba or say other
things like   inverted wish please find
nectar there in that flower not
yet bloomed

CARTOGRAPHER'S LOVE POEM

i can never be the one who
says that he loves you like the
grace of leaves   palest green
even in october
but the poet needs me just the same
i take his love and press
line upon line of it into tight and tighter curves
turn what is wider than night   a poet's love
and give it scale

i cannot tell you why a river loves the sea
and loses its name to some other river
that also loves the sea
and is therefore like passion
but i can tell you that the
nile   danube   volga and ob
if strung together are 11,615 miles
and that must mean something
about love

i also cannot   weave anything   not pain
as a metaphor of braiding hair
over under over under and through and so on
but i can point to a small place   g-11
just north of that river and east of that town
you loved her and it did not work
i   because i am kind   have marked that spot
placed it   right at the fold of the map
so that you will not always hurt

i will never mark the groan
of the feverfew tasted at by four hummingbirds
but i can draw for you   her body
a meadow between two hills beneath three waterfalls
next to a smudge of green   the way i say forest
where the lines of the map tighten to almost touching
a mountain laid flat for your finger to trace
to imagine how fast those four
hummingbird hearts must beat

MAN FALLS FROM GREAT DISTANCE   WRITES POEM

light years from her
he falls through ancient echoes of radio traffic
among the audible fossils of longing he cries
hello hello is there anyone out there

just me just me   like a comet hurling itself toward you
he is unaware of the irony of this comet
how it will be visible centuries and centuries
before she hears the trailing echo of how he loves her

he falls   pulled by gravity
through the ribbon light of
two stars   dead for 15,000 years
he understands

this light   its luminescence   its patience
how it exists in the deep whisper of space
how it longs
and why it dies

he plummets past eight moons of saturn
the delicate bones of a celestial wrist
phoebe hyperion enceladus five others
remnants of some creation

he knows they are the pearls from scripture
removed from the flesh where
God created love
the reason for his falling

after much falling he falls some more
always toward the profound pull of her gravity
he promises   there in the deep cold
that he will burn across the sky for her

he proclaims that each galaxy is a bright
trail of his descent   that the innumerable
things she calls stars are each
an abacus bead marking every second he has loved her

for her he falls through
auroras of charged light
toward the sweet curve of the earth
that swallows light whole

he loves her wrists   his eyes orbit them
like planets he has passed   like moons
he has passed like satellites he has
passed   like a prayer of arcing light

to reach her he falls with
green brown and blue rivers plunging into sky
he falls just to breathe his love against
the cliffs of her skin

he falls over the plunge of many rivers
and there he flutters
before again falling
a great distance

he falls further still
past a man on a tightrope who nods knowingly

she is the breeze that presses on them
he imagines her wrist

the soft hinge   the angel of her hand
the quiver of wind
that trembles with him
in the final seconds of his falling

he dreams the two of them together
recounts his fall through spirals of galaxies
past auroras of light
among dead and dying stars

orbiting with many moons and planets
he dreams himself tasting at her lips
he dreams how his love   bright as twin suns
might break his fall

Ricky (still) loves Lulu
for Chris Ransick

i love her eyes   their green and faint brown
which reminds me of our home   the places
where river meets llano and maybe this   unto itself
is another definition of love   i imagine
her flute upon the saints and silent
congregation   each lost among their own prayers

i think of my friend Chris   his wife ill
a move to the sea that will help stave off
what the mountains and wind
bring more quickly than ocean
friends offer them secular prayers
and i do not know what those are

i only know the prayers
of old ladies or hands pressed
together like two perfect five fingered bodies
prayers of repetition   hesitation
and the press of longing in the voice
where even the silent "dear God" has its aching

twenty years ago i saw a spray painted
overpass proclamation   *Ricky loves Lulu*
i thought   he must love her so much   to dangle there
above the freeway   a love struck batman
later   the proper authorities of such things
erased their names with silver paint   but

Ricky returned   added *still*
to his profession of love and faith and
this must be what my friends are calling
secular prayers   the *still* of   *Ricky still loves Lulu*
the constancy of *still* is perhaps what
they intend with those prayers i don't know or understand

i wonder if he persists   if he continues to
love Lulu   i wonder if he would leave his life   the
stillness he has grown into   leave it all for Lulu
move to the humid and thick sea or the gasping desert
realizing   finally   that his life is her
this epiphany   really   all he needs to know

his was an act of a young person   has age ruined
what he believed perfect   i wonder
what thoughts entered as he took his red paint
to the overpass   did he say   with this gesture
i promise to protect you   to hold you when people
around you lose the compass of sympathy and decency

did he say   Lulu i promise to drive to the
store at any hour for whatever you need   i promise
to be a good man   to chop wood and light a fire
of sweet smelling pinon when you are cold
to call because i love your voice before you say goodbye
as if   perhaps   our parting is imagined before it is spoken

Ricky loves Lulu   and later   Ricky still loves Lulu
how long can *still* remain true

how long can his seven words wrestle out from
beneath the paint that attempts to erase his claims
pushing   like a silvery death trying
to kill what must remain true   still

IF WE NEVER MET

i am sure i would dream you
and therefore love you

my dream eyes would trace the slow
river of your spine to where
it meets with the
small of your back
and there i would find
the sweet crescent of your skin
at its confluence with another
river of fresh raw honey

and if we never met
on the shores of lake geneva
i would love you in the shadow
of your left eye
i would love you like a thousand bees
in a field with tamarisk and i
would trace the invisible map
of your eye's shadow toward your lips
toward the softness of your belly
and the falling water of your voice
the place where i would love you
if we never met

and if we never met
i would love you in the place
arabs call sahel
the shore between the african

desert and the african grasslands
i would pass you unannounced
in the unknowing sahel of our lives

something inside of us
would begin to count
at that moment when we did not meet
and the two of us
would know
that time is measured in seconds
only by those without love

because we never met
we would invent a new time
and call it the shore between
our passing and our meeting
we would measure it
with the slowly struck note of a piano
the wonderful pause
between the sound and the moment
the music leaves the listener
that is where i would love you
if we never met

and if we never met
i would love you like the scientist
who claims that if two people
never meet then there is no chance
they shall ever meet and
therefore in the order of things
not change the world

i would love you like the scientist
and fill notebooks full of
formulas where i solve and solve
to prove you exist and so too
love me

in my scientist's heart there would
be great equations
where divinity swims freely
equations that make us possible
and explain how in our passing
we have already connected
like a chime of thunder
knotted with a string of lightning

and if we never met
i would find you
in the sahel of our lives
where nomads seek well water
in the far corners of a field
where a bush blooms pink and red
if we never met i would find you
in the shadows of your sight
on a distant lake's shore
to the right of the equal sign

i can promise you
that if we never met
i would find you
and therefore love you
i would

AS MY LOVE SPEAKS

the brain is like a map of Africa: still largely uncharted
—Barbet Schroeder

the place i try and hold you in
is like a map of africa   largely uncharted
and this poem   this poem
the way your voice
though i love it more than
the fire of a bird's wing
this poem   a love poem
will be a great distance from beautiful
because your voice
is gravity   and i
i fall like oats from an open hand
wondering how your next word
might then make me fall
into the prolonged blink
of your concentration

i am a lost nomad
on the old salt roads
across the desert   i
do not dare map the place
i love you in
my finger so barely
touching your elbow
uncharted place
your skin   where so barely there
echo   your voice

persists   gravity
deep deep water
i cannot drink
and if only for the moment
when you pause between words
i imagine how knowing
your next thought might
save me forever

1,017,900 POUNDS

every day thirty trains pass through el paso
the trains are five hands of five different railways
that follow the green border of river trees
the weight of one engine is 581,400 pounds
and 436,500 for a fully loaded tender
but when there is too much weight

he returns to the miracle of his five fingers   weightless
hummingbirds that hover over the passage
where trains carry like pacific waves   tender
images of parallel lives   the railways
are two hands never meeting   two wishes never pounding
two bodies never touching   windblown trees

and yes in this metaphor two desert willow trees
on two sides of the rio grande both wait
he for his juarez Beatrice and she for the pounding
thump of a guitarron from a well lit house in el paso
later the music will follow her in many ways
like leaning trees that do not touch   almost tender

she will not know the tenderness
plucked notes of old love songs diminishing in april trees
that grow among switching yards and railways
he guides trains in with a lantern   one flame without weight
inexhaustible blue flame   hottest where the light passes
through cloudy glass   the lantern weighs 16 ounces

the lantern   a pendulum which rhythmically pounds
the lantern   his heart   an empty room where he is the tender
each day his lantern heart beats over 100,000 times in el paso
in juarez she listens but guesses it is only the trees
the way they rustle and lean as if bent by the weight
of the motionless trains blooming from the railways

there are five paired lines and each railway
a place where nothing is measured in kilos or pounds
where love forgets gravity   prayer has no weight
a prayer that is more patient than mountains   a tender
prayer that flutters like butterflies in pine trees
a prayer that recalls no border   no jaurez   no el paso

he will always wait for her among the trees   the railways
that carry engines and tenders that weigh 1,017,900 pounds
a glance from his love will float away all the trains in el paso

TWO LIONS HUNTED THE PLAINS OF AFRICA
for M & M after a trip to the Field museum in chicago

there were two lions
who hunted men on the plains of africa

my love is two silent lions moving past
fires and thorns meant to keep them out

the lions are the tips of my fingers
they would kill grown men to

only once
trace your skin

these two lions are gold
in a field of gold grass

there were two lions that
hunted as a pair on the plains of africa

the first of these lions disappears
when you speak   the other stops to

drink sun warm water when
you smile

my love is two lions stuck
silent and glass eyed in a chicago museum

my lions hunt for you nightly
the two loves never leave their glass cage

the two lions
are chambers of my heart

they have tracked you
since you first arrived

the men on the plains of africa
named the lions

ghost and darkness
these two lions are my love

the world builds bridges
away from where the lions hunt

two lions that equal my love
find your scent nightly

two lions that equal my love
will be killed by a hunter

their frail skins will
be sent to chicago

where a silent man will
reconstruct their bodies

two african lions
equal my love

there is a section of a chicago
museum dedicated to my love

my love is two african lions
with glass eyes

my love is frozen
by a hunter's bullet

my love
two lions

rests behind
clear and frozen glass

there were two african lions
that hunted on the plains of africa

these lions
are my love

you pass daily
in front of the lions

the lions will themselves to move
the lions cannot

you float away from the lions
you are a reflection on glass

two lions dare follow
two lions without end are frozen and cannot

my love is two gold lions
in a field of gold

THE SEVEN STARS VISIBLE

should be
red as mars

as though my wishes
depended upon

two things touching
the sigh of contact

where your body
heals me   and the

apple becomes
prophecy   rather than sin

THE EARTH AT NIGHT   YOUR BODY

as i orbit you i begin to love you
and perhaps you are cairo
blooming at the edge of things
the dark desert and the ribbon light of the nile

in the middle of the sahara
there is a place that nomads call tenere
which in their language means nothingness
it is like the deep pause between the stars

i am this small satellite
the first to love you
your spinning makes me possible
physicists say that i am constantly falling

my orbit over the earth at night   your body
will always be made of three syllables
tenere nothingness satellite perigee apogee
i love you picayune sleeping land emptiness

yet i glide over your skin
trace the dark blue and greens of your night
find fires where no one has ever lived
find slow and soft blue where glaciers glow back at me

because i love you i orbit you   map your light
and in my constant night you burn so beautifully
moscow a perfect star   st. petersburg your dim sister
always you are cairo or some other constant burning

your oceans repeat against your ribs
this is where you glow turquoise in my night
your shining body delivered up to me
your satellite

sometimes   my love
i orbit only to know the infinite dark green
of siberia whose name means
sleeping land

there i find your deepest lake
whose name has no origin
perhaps lake baikal
is your heart

three hundred rivers flow in
only the angara flows away
might i be   i can never be
this river flowing through siberia

dear and beautiful earth at night
you have so many names
i want to know the origins of all your places
know the source of every river

in the deep curve
of your hips
i will mine for salt
and name that place taudenni

your navel
i'll orbit there
perhaps forever
name it the congo

your lips   i'll find a place
where orchids always grow
and i will call this place
nombre de dios

when i am closest to you
it will be called perigee
your hand almost in mine
i'll name this distance picayune

and then i will spin away
toward my apogee
i will name this place something simple
punta arenas

i will give you innumerable names
all of them filled with vowels
all of them like pearls
always something like cairo

and someday your gravity
will pull me from this orbit
and your body   the earth
will burn me to ash

perhaps i will burn across the sky
where two lovers in an empty field
can watch me glow and burn into you
my earth   they will aaahh at the way i love you

FOR CENTURIES AND SO ON

it's true
i did not know
i had loved you for centuries

distant blue
beneath the blue   you
beneath blue   you

beyond you
a mound of dirt beneath
a snow that will not stick

a soft rise of earth
a house where centuries ago
I loved you

fallen house
soft earth mound
that used to be the house

beyond the house a woodpile
further beyond a river
beyond the woodpile a river

we are smoke
we are made of smoke
the two of us made of smoke

might i repeat myself
i didn't know
that i've loved you for centuries

river bend into another bend
which bends and bends again
against rocks where someone carved us into stone

look   you are the river on stone and i
i am that hand   a left hand of stone
a finger made of stone four others of feathers

i've loved you for centuries
for centuries i've loved you
you   for centuries   love

until now   an october
an october on the edge of november
october on november's edge   i didn't know until now

river bend into soft earth   a home
distant blue   you   perfect wood which burns all night
my hand is feathers   you   a river on stone

you ask the perfect question
how long have you loved me
is the perfect question you ask

i answer since we first touched
our first touch i answer since then
since we touched for the first time

something as still as stone
stillness like stone   something
with a stillness of stone says   no

perhaps the sky paused between trees
the trees have paused the sky
perhaps where the sky has paused between trees

something like silent stones or sky between trees
silent stone   pause of sky
tells me not since first we touched

for centuries that's how long
bend in the river sweetly bend into another
bend and sweetly so bend and so on that's how long

THE CALCULUS OF YOU

a balloon is rising at the rate of 5ft/s
a boy is cycling along a straight road at a speed of 15ft/s
when he passes under the balloon it is 45 ft above him
how fast is the distance between the balloon
and the boy increasing 3 seconds later

something inside of me says to solve for X
where X is the distance
between the boy and the balloon
and i am the boy and you are
the balloon and therefore Y

i must set both to 0 because i
am looking for something 3 seconds
from now   like a moment after you
turn away but before the perpetuity
of the instant before you leave

i wonder stupid things
like what color is my bike
and of course it matters
what season we are in because
i somehow love you more in spring

yes   the road is straight
but is it paved
i know it can't be
because our love is old and sometimes ·
i compare it to the moon

in short   there are too
many variables to the
way i love you   so
i wonder is this really
a love poem

you   after all are ascending away
from me at a rate which has been
determined to be 5 ft/sec and therefore
15 feet further away 3 seconds
after i began chasing you

me   i'm traveling at 15 ft/sec
which means i am moving
faster than you   which
insures that this is
in fact   a love poem

because i've also
read about the horizon
and something forgiving
inside of me also whispers
gravity

this is just another
way for me to say
that i love you
and though it is longing now
i ride   i ride

i ride so that i
will hold you
somewhere in a spring field
whose specks of green
are barely visible

but this doesn't answer
how fast the distance between
the boy and the balloon is increasing
so i remind myself of the horizon
of gravity   of how much i love you

so that my love becomes
something like this   where
distance is called D
though D is temporary
and because this is still calculus

we divide the temporary by how
fast i am pedaling and factor in
the rotation of the earth
and i love the earth too because it
makes what i am about to say possible

the distance of the balloon
multiplied by spring   divided by
the dirt road factored into
the earth's spinning which is 800 mph
because i'm not at the equator

is just another way of
saying that i am riding my bike
because i love you
and in case you care i've made my heart
into a metronome to pace my pedaling

i know my professor will mark this wrong
but by my calculations
you   the balloon   and me
the boy   are not getting
further apart

in fact   i've determined that you
will enter into my arms
at pt Z in exactly
the time it takes for me
to pedal there

TWO RIVERS NEXT TO WHICH I WOULD LOVE YOU   AND HOW

i
zambezi zambezi
slow calm zambezi
deep slow calm
zambezi soft deep
river fall
in rainbows fall
your voice   sweet
zambezi zo zo zo zambezi
calm slow zambezi
your voice your voice
taste you on my tongue
zambezi zambezi over
this cliff and that
edge   zambezi
deep zambezi calm slow
zambezi fall and fall
then calm slow deep   fall again
zambezi   taste you
slow deep river
on my tongue

ii
urubamba tumble roll
tumble roll urubamba
tumble roll shift tumble
shape   rumble shift tumble
shape roll tumble canyons
shape roll urubamba roll so

tumble bamba you
sweet bamba sweet cool urubamba
my cup   my cup
this cup   please please
uru   bamba u   ru
lose your name in
the jungle tumble
roll   tumble shift still
uru   bamba
u bamba u uru
u bamba you bamba
uru you tumble
bamba u ru bamba
roll shift   fill my cup
'til all your syllables
grow still

I HAVE FOR A MOMENT

always loved you
and that is the easiest thing i
have ever said

in the distant 6:00 a.m. fog
there is a curve
of a mountain

or is it a small city
glowing orange and pink
against the fog

i pray
my hands barely touch
i say amen

that space
the delicate breath
between my hands

in the almost image
of a mountain
in the pink and orange glow

i have in those
and every moment
always loved you

and that
is the easiest
thing i have ever said

LOVE POEM ON STONE

i've loved her
perhaps not like i should have
but more like the specks of white
thinnest and scattered salt
blended into this stone

she is the blade of grass
from scripture
the green and crescent hand
of the river whose sweat
she rolled into this stone

this stone whose river voice
has kissed at the edges of me
bent itself slowly
into the shape of
this stone

red stone   small corazon
of shadow where the river of
her right hand   her skin
thumbs fingers thumbs
caresses this stone

smooth stone   work stone
that is the way i
should have loved her
like a slow rolling that brings
her scent into the wind

TEETER

near you
i am a table
with one uneven leg

i wish someone
you perhaps
would place a

bottle cap
folded napkins
a sheaf of poems

beneath my damaged places
a touch
that ends my teetering

LIKE HERMES AT THE EDGE OF A FIELD

he watches cranes dance
each like a silvery star
as the world bends itself
toward the green of may
remembers how   from their dance
hermes invented the alphabet
how cranes made this poem possible

he knows that all unseen things
have their earthly shape
how forgiveness   the softness of it
is the muzzle of a horse
and he knows too   that a wish
is a task for many birds
for each crane   a purpose

take for example   his wish for love
how one crane   its body like
awkward mercury loosed upon
a field of wasted grain
takes flight   seeks music
until there is too much
sound for one heart to thank

while another crane flies off
a flute running   leaping into
an etude of april night
each note each breath a phase of moon
while another crane finds itself
on the jet stream of wishes where
his mind falls down her thigh

crane upon crane
this one like an auger
cleaving away at the
broken parts of her
this one to the guff of wishes
to pluck the treed fruit
into a great basket of a greater wish

this crane to divert her thoughts
a river toward an ocean
it didn't know it was intended to meet
and this crane like a cello
groaning into the morning sky
because of all the loves
it is the cello that most remembers the tree

a wish is the work of many birds
a flock of cranes each of them
a single letter carried in the
whistle hollow bones of their wings
until in a windy spring   as they dance
love finds the wisher
seven cranes spelling her name

TOUCH AND VOICE

the soft flame of it
her touch
unties me
like a ribbon

prayers from an
alphabet of rain
her voice
that too   unravels me

GOOD FRIDAY

here is one of those prayers
one of those prayers that
falls and falls and
comes like spring

in the valley
the world is gold
the sun moves across the page
of the southern sky

the silhouette of a woman
on an eastbound bus
the sun makes her real
casts her image against the window

she holds a
newborn level with her eyes
her silhouette and the baby
she coos to must be spring

i'm searching really
i long for anything green
some sign of life
that isn't born of wind

i've heard one of those
rumors that there are
cherry blossoms in bloom
i long for anything pink   red or white

here there is gold   tall gold grass
and what of that gold horse
the palomina with the blue halter
i long for something blue

good friday
two horses run to the fence
to greet the peregrinos
marching toward the church

one horse with a black mane
the other   gold as the grass
both of them try to speak to us
their winter coats caught color

a red mare
her winter coat blinks
red black red red red on black
flashes as snow moves in from the east

have you ever
seen a horse's eyes
galaxies and nebulae of brown
grow in their eyes

sun hits the gold horse
snow begins to fall
both rest themselves on the palomina
she is made gold and white

this woman i love
she too is spring
i love her like a river rising
i love her like spring rising

her eyes
i long for something green
her eyes and the hint
of leaves being born on the cottonwoods

i love her like leaves being born
i love her
like a strong wind
through thick cottonwood

i love her like
spring rising in the river
like trees along
a river rising

in my prayer
she sings
in the deep red of the
human voice

in spanish she sings
of la primavera   four syllables
in spanish our love
is made of four syllables

our love is made
of four vowels
i long for anything made of sun or
four syllables   four vowels
i know she knows my prayer
i want her voice to sing
for her eyes to construct the
words my prayer is made of

CRANE POEM FOR MY LOVE

two cranes fly west
into a snowy march morning
these two cranes
mates for life will both
outlive us
and one day my love
because their wings are powerful
because they are the highest
flying of all the symbols of love
one day
my love
these two birds will
deliver us to the
place the chinese call
western paradise
they are called xian he
heavenly bird
bird of happiness

because it is custom
i will draw them with
tortoises
bamboo
stone
symbols of long life
for us my love
i wish us something
permanent as cranes

and because cranes
know all the gods
if one of us should
lets not say it
but if
one of us should
then the gods will send
either you or i
to this mortal place
and one of us will
trumpet into the morning air
one of us will dance
among the wasted grain
in the farmer's field

for you my love
if i'm first
i will throw feathers into the sky
i will pray my crane prayer
in the early dawn
for you
if i'm first
i will stand with my head
buried in my wing
one leg raised up to my body
i will
for you
stand that way
so you can see that
only the tips of my wings
are black
there is only that much

sadness

if i should

lets not say it

only the tips of
my wings will be sad
the rest of me will
burn white and red
white and red my love
i'll wait in my red and
white vigilance
i will wait

in myth the crane
lives for a thousand years
and there are stories
of how emperors
loved them
there are stories of prayers
tied to the leg of a crane
so the crane might
deliver the fallen

how will you
if
lets not

but if i'm left
i will think of
cranes   for you my love

my prayer
when you read it
will be in symbol

for centuries
poets have loved cranes
i will write
how god visits earth
flown down to us
on the backs of cranes

for my love i will write
a crane poem
that lives in two worlds
one thin line
for every crane
flying into an autumn sky
and yet another line
for each crane
returning to a river's source
and another line
for the crane song that tells
peasants to sow their fields

when i finish these lines
the poem will fall from
the sky of continents
and while the crane sleeps
i will tie a prayer poem
to its leg
for god
to carry back

to you
my love
my xian he
heavenly bird
a poem
a prayer
like this one
for you

THE FISHERMAN'S SONG OF DESPAIR OR *ONCORHYNCUS MYKISS*

in my trout dream
you are twin to the dawn
the pearl of your belly
that is the sky in the

brief breaths   the moments
of sunless light   a wash of pink
guazing at the center of you
ghosting away at your caudal edges

and in the human chamber
of my heart   where it
hilts up against the primal
and the uncharted

i assume that on the fifth day
God had grown weary and therefore
created you to perfect
the domes and orbits that preceded you

so that every possible
sky might be foretold
there upon
your wet body

this shadowless light
milks its white breath
against the river   and there
in the riffles and the deep pools

the trout queue themselves
in a braid of shadows
they are the movement of dreams
what man looked upon when he created music

randomly
consistently as the slow dreams
where i hold you
i remember that the phoenicians

had an alphabet
the egyptians   written words
but neither was blessed enough to
have written your name   to have

held you in the God light of dawn
and what of that fourth chamber
the one whose room
has flooded and is yours

the dead trees along the river
have forgotten what they are
everything is part wish
part shadow   this indescribable light

of madrugada rubbing itself
against this river   and i should not have
touched you   and because of you
dreamt of rain or a slope of trees or

a moonlit snowstorm or a ribbon
of stars landed and touchable
your body a constellation
to my wishes

spilling back into the river
toward the secret spot of the human body
the haunt of you
barely there in my hand

JUDYTH HILL

All Journeys Have Secret Destinations
of which
the Traveler Is Unaware.

—*Martin Buber*

JUDYTH HILL

What a gift! Not only to assemble a collection of new poems, but to stutter and stammer towards an Ars Poetica, a rumination of my own!

Here's a try: poetry is an impassioned lightening strike of language, a storm in the heart, in the mind, in the blood. It's the rain we long to stand out in, splash, get drenched, dry ourselves by the fire, quiet, later, fresh words on white paper, scent of wet.

It's reciprocal echo; a calling to and back from this so utterly amazing world, this very gracious state we inhabit, known as alive...

Or maybe this: It's the itch, the heat, the build-up of electrical charges condensed out of the real & imaginary weather of our lives.

When the push, pulse, the tender, the grim, the unjust, the exquisite can't be contained any more, it is released, groundward, in a distillation of cadence and *le mot juste*.

That's a mouthful!

Wordsworth wrote: "Poetry is the spontaneous overflow of powerful feelings: it takes its origin from emotion recollected in tranquility."

So, ahh: maybe poetry is the dead calm of the sea, it's the well-trimmed sailboat in irons, holding and containing that heart-rending still point. Then: prepare to come about!

Or a pot of honeyed Earl Grey, aromatic and full, and so easily, we tip over and write.

William Carlos Williams posited a poem as, "A small (or large) machine made of words", adding, "There can be no part, as in any other machine, that is redundant".

Aha! That cool cowboy, craft, comes a ridin' into town, spinning all the ladies in a swift two-step, knockin' back his whiskey, neat, and winning at poker with his unflinching gaze, aces and eights up his sleeve.

Make it look easy, but kiddo, make it.

Trust that your craft will stay mysteriously by your side, and enter, stage left, when needed.

But, still...why poetry?

Lucille Clifton said, "A bird doesn't sing because he has answers. He sings because he has a song."

Born to it. Got to. Just lucky, I guess.

Poetry doesn't have to "work", the ferociously misused word of poetry workshops. Poetry doesn't need a job.

The Bard has a job. The Bard has to stop being busy. The Bard has to ask after your Aunt Sophie, and notice the first velvety buds of the scrub oaks in late March, that exact green like none other. The Bard gets to listen to all the good gossip, the crunch of tires on gravel, owls scquack, and the hush after wind sweeps through the canyon ponderosa.

Then sing it back to the people, storied alive, replete with seasons and phases of the moon, the flavor of apricots, your best kiss and the aroma of toast that morning, in language you have given your all to...

Poetry is the exultant state of the ecstatically unemployed who work like lilies and iron workers, hard and gorgeously.

It's the best non-work I've ever done. Poetry is the way in, the way out.

The gift I got, a dowry at birth; like my mother's silver and her sorrow, knowing to put salt in the soup, and her voice, still vivid so many years later, reading us to sleep:

> "The sun did not shine it was too wet to play, so we sat in the house all that cold wet day, I sat there with Sally we sat there we two and I said how I wish we had something to do..."

Turning to Virgil and dactylic hexameter, scanning iambics, sonnets and sestinas. Left rhyme and meter at 14, wrote the black angst ridden poems of adolescence, lots of zealous poems on Viet Nam and boyfriends.

Always in love with words... just head over heels for pure sound, a serious crush on soft vowels, mouth open; teased by the cool click of consonant. Poetry has great mouth feel, like Double Bubble, it's elastic and tensile, like Haagen Daz, it's silky and creamy, like New Mexico's beloved green chile, it's picante: poignantly hot and sweet, and your eyes tear and tear.

Then the turn-on of getting passionate about exact.

Poetry is threshold, entrance and exit to the Morada, that place of mystery, the tender, raw, household of faith.

The celebrants, secret, but kin to hummingbird and bear, moth and musk ox, sworn to brother/sisterhood, wrestling to articulate the aching to be said—or is it heard?

Where does the urge originate? I think we are both the knight and the fair maiden, the catcher and the caught.

Sometimes it's pure call: the heart's *shofar*, summoning us, not to understand, but to stand under, make relation, to dare hold steady in wonder.

And sometimes poem is an unknown horizon we struggle towards, wrapped in the cloak of invisibility, wearing seven league boots we have stolen and which pull us now relentlessly forward.

Poet Jack Mueller told me, "Obey emergent form", and deliciously, "Be ambushed by the ambush". Whichever way poem is happening, chased or chasing, these are tools I keep in the top shelf of the tool box, critical as duct tape and baling wire.

Poetry is my way of impassioned, diligent, beauty making; singing, as best I can on any given day, the world to good. But never at the expense of the poem.

Jean Cocteau: "The poem, like the moon must advertise nothing". The poem has no axe to grind, no sales pitch to make.

In prose, good prose, we go forward, but in poetry, verse, verso, we must turn and turn. And ride, heart in our mouth, the curling wave of that turning towards what is true. Poetry can live with its own confusion, if you say it clearly.

What else will cut you that good a deal?

WOW! Too good. Makes you reel.

Poetry is the small I, the big WE. It's the scent of the imaginary wafting off the sensuous curves of real bread. The Everything Matters School: my alma mater.

Poetry is charm bracelet, linking our connection to the cheetah, the red tail, Pascal flowers and botryoidal slopes of malachite.

It's factoids and figures and your Nana's chicken soup, and her recipe for matzoh balls, and it's none of those.

Forget yourself! Then remember!

It's the self firing just right with the world, a good oxygen mix.

It's simple: and not. It's the gift economy's distributary function; you give because you have: that's how abundance is created and spread: artists not as "gifted" but gifting.

Poetry wants to make a sound in the world; we need to be the first ears on the scene.

It's the right in the body, out of your mind, straight from the heart real thing.

Sylvia Plath said, "Poetry is the blood jet"; I say, it's the lifeline.

Alice Waters wrote, "Every poem is a thank you letter, an IOU and a complaint to the management".

I say, write on.

This Will Find You Ready

"Go I know not where,
To get I know not what"
Parsival, Wolfgang Von Escherbach

When you lose everything, then you track.

This world is always spinning,
on chicken legs, at the edge of the forest.
You will need each chip of obsidian, every flake of flint,
all caught parts of conversations,

glimpses of clematis behind fences in hidden courtyards.
Remember a soaker rain, trill of orioles at first light.

Every scent of hyacinth, of jasmine, is a vow,
every birdsong, the call to prayer,
a rooftop in another city, but always your own.

Call in all the magic.
Set a place at your table, silver knives, fishbones,
chess pieces of ancient ivory.

Can you see it? You've been so many times.

You've been the one who kneads the bread,
 the one who comes to the table in sackcloth,
the one who sits beside the king, in aquamarine and emerald.
The crown, the crow, the crone.
It is all the same.

This time bring the sword,
This blade strikes once and once only.
Ask for leave, and do one thing right,
It's all you can do.

You must ask your question.

Permission will be given in both worlds.

But, there is a second chance:
at least in this story.

Tell it the old way, aloud.
Build a fire of the nine woods gathered, apple, hawthorn, hazel,
willow, rowan, vine and fir.

You already know. You have done this.

You will make what you desire appear, by your own seeking,
by your willingness
to sing as you approach,
to walk slowly, to keep going,

to serve what you walk towards with your whole,
broken,
wild heart.

Mermaid Dreaming Fish Into Diatonic Scales

"Drieman", meaning "to make music", Is the earliest word for dream in Old English
"Butango", meaning, "One with the star gods", is the Zulu word for sleep

Twelve clocks in circular ticking is dream music.
I say moon, in Vedic hand signals.
Every mudra is a recipe for bread.
Yeast is birdsong - a leavening that starts us daily.

When I rise, it is into hilarity and crescendo of green forest.

I pine for you, beloved.
You taught me vertical, as in Hazelrod,
and most certainly, horizontal...

In a circle of 300 mysteries,
I translate myself into the wisdom of salmon
and sweet nut meats.
Re-imagine the alphabet of lichen,
at the miraculous visit of stag and doe.

I count by color: Indigo,
Sterling knight, larkspur, and faerybells
heard in a number between seven and nine.

I learn this by touch, taste the inventive possibility of clematis
in the arms of honeysuckle,
an embrace of sentient fragrance.
Brew tea and sip.

Heat is the clavicle of the morning dove,
what bones know, first shine returned of eclipsed crescent.
The yielding back into our eyes, you in my arms.

Bedtime is a story of woodpecker and willow wave,
a map drawn by bee dance, whirr of mixer in dough,
long strands we develop by knead and push,
one foot on the ground, one resting forward, towards next time,
door to our secret hearts thoroughly open.

Light a fire in the horno, when the heat turns paper
a color practiced by live oak,
we'll make love, I mean,
bread.

Thirst Is For Knowing Water

Drink this.

Moons spin and whirl in the offworlds of the heart.
Such water as I carry is his, by worth, by curve
of smile and horizon.

In dream, he lifted the cup, saying, *Drink this,*

I tasted the wild sage of Grenada,
fireflies in a veil of evening,
the kissed stones of Mecca.
Monarch butterflies in flight 3 generations,
knowing no origin but desire.

My thirst is that migration, that carried cup, that shiver,
fever, cloud.
He is mirror, door, whisper, fire, husky-tongued moonlight.

This thirst is not for quenching,
but for drowning in.

I offer my body's secret body
to the Dark One.
The wind in the piney canyon
is tonight, his voice,
strong and musical, under Lyra and the Scales,
 the Lion Rampant.

Drink this,

I do and taste sovereignty
inside this surrender.

Flickers take wing, over hills, over ridgeline,
I follow
crossing thresholds
to his bed,
scent of honeysuckle and wetland.

Judyth says, I listen closely
to the voice of the Beloved.

From the seed of one dropped decibel,
mountains rise, inside his cadence,
fresh rivers spring.

FIRST STEPS

In Centro, children skitter in curbside push-pull.
Evening translates into *Iglesia*.
I become lucid in bells, bilingual in apse and nave.
I look always for love, buy tin horse-drawn toys,
all gleam and spin.

I have come somewhere rich in *carnitas* and happenstance,
a wealth of tortillas maize, and *escobas*, sweeping, sweeping.
Leaves scatter and fall on cobblestone, their dip and roll,
round rock roads, and steep.
I walk and lose myself ever easily, in luxurious tilt.

It is effortless, this vanish.
I cross cultures and corners, and never see anything twice.
Have two languages to forget in.
All my verbs in the present tense.

You have lost me, or I, you.
It hardly matters, I earn my confusion honestly.
Last light on the coral spires of the *Parrochia*,
Looking, as ever, an elaborate wedding cake for God.

I want to marry God, that's why I have come, some hope of co-habitation
in the household of Holy.
It's here, and I am too.

Between the resound of horns, bessos, and blessings,
mucho gustos and bay laurel press shoulder to shoulder in the *Jardin*.
Mariachis play, and this is real, I promise.

I live in Mexico, and have no idea how I came to do such a thing.

My own life shocks me.
I dress always oddly and can't find streets I've walked for years in dreams,
Everywhere so nearly familiar.

I do have a grammar of clocktime, could parse
the yesterday that led me here: to a bench facing
southwest and beatific, baskets of zinnias and girasols,
to *elotes*, dripping *mantequilla* and red chile,
Michoacán ices in white paper cups
with soft folds,
sweet *refrescos*, and you.

There's legitimacy in my wandering.
When have I ever known where I am, anyway?
Finally, I surrender.
Become buoyant with happiness, remember the secret of being lost:
Stay still, wait
To be found.

Cielito Lindo, the music reminds,
and the sun strikes a luminous bargain of warmth on rose walls.
Maps are not needed.
This is where an archangel lives, and the future.
That is enough direction for one night.

How I Got Here

By ochre stain and auroch horn, and the words for things I don't know
looked up in the OED, by Greek roots, and Indo-Scyth,
paintings on the cave walls in Catal Hüyük and the secret
burial mounds in Anatolia. I got here by the gold in the Altai,
and the *ea* diphthong:
Learn   Teach   Wheat   Death   Fear   Ocean   Tea   Heaven
The standing stones in Waterval Boven,
the Uffizi and the Aya Sofya,
and Cincinnati, the only place I really did go.
I got here by a preserve of white lions, 6 phases of the moon,
my daughter's eyes,
my son's practiced grip on the rockface of steep.
I got here by chocolate soufflés and new boxes of Crayola 64.
Privilege and poverty in equal measure.
1968, Stokley, Malcolm, and Martin. Marches
on Washington and Union Square,
and The Tooth Mother Naked at Last.
The Stones got me here, and Otis, BB and Pat Metheny. Tinarawin,
Ali Farka. Bessie and Billie.
Ella and Louie kept me here, and the Gospel according
to Rodgers and Hammerstein.
And my mother's night cracked voice: Mack the Knife and lullabies.
By footfalls echoing in the hushed halls of the Natural History:
Paleolithic and Pacific Northwest, totems and canoes,
the Rothkos in the National Gallery, Wollman's rink,
My tiny black skirt. Guernica at the Modern.
The Henry Moore and Calder's youknowwhere..
I got here by vodka and crisis and blue irises opening
in another woman's vase.

By 300 CPW, double lattes, osso buco, Meyer's lemons,
sashimi, pastrami on rye, forks on the left, knife on the right,
Chinese on Sunday nights, potstickers, steamed, not fried.
Cloth napkins. Dial soap and Fresca.
I got here by days and days of double-bills in the Thalia:
Children of Paradise, Breathless,
Surs les Toits du Paris, Black Orpheus, Jacque Tati, Z, and the sound
of slow zippers.
By amber and amethyst and my Grandmother's graduated pearls lost
in Taos Hot Springs.
By the last fluorite from the Annabel Lee mine, by the ivory elephants
Papa brought back from India,
which my father gave me, even though I lose everything.
I got here by losing everything.
I got here by a '66 Plymouth Valiant, slant six engine,
And the 85 Dodge Colt I rolled in the Galisteo night.
Bad Bird 101, the scars you can't see.
I almost didn't get here by the cranky 2nd gear of my 92 Toyota Previa,
The car my lawyers got, 287,000 miles later.
I got here by duct tape and baling wire, by MAC Out To Sea eyeliner,
too many adjectives, T.S. Eliot and astonishment.
By wildgrasses, lack of dog and presence of cat,
By my apple trees in final bloom.
By the way I'll never see you again in this life,
And the road I took to make that true.

Night of River's Filling: A Crown of Sonnets

Let me not to the marriage of true minds...
create dissonance. The curve-billed thresher, in her mockingbird life
sings lonely. You answer: Marry me, my heart has the fragrance
of sweet acacia, scent of spring's first flower. We could,
if we so loved, grow past prickle into poppy's tender petal,
find our way past *garambullo*'s arboled sting,
walk the Presa's new shoreline, edged with fresh silt.
I'll hold your hand, if you let me near.
I promise my eyes to this land, to be the wind through *palo dulce*.
You be the branches that entangle against night.
I say, each morning, Beloved, let us try
to listen back the song of the one that has no nest,
yet waits patient for the one who'll love her best.

Wait patient for the one that loves her best,
a time short that time itself recalls.
I came here willing, and willing will remain, whether here or not.
I've said yes to everything offered: doors become views and later, paintings
of landscapes lost, hang in new rooms. Shouldn't there be a museum
for the parts
our hearts break into?
For what we can remember and do? Collect the lost and broken limbs of
the Ancients there. Winged Victory might look like this: what we can
piece together, a near fit.
And the chance to be whole, wholly desired. Buy a ticket to the next stop:
I always wanted to stay, I did.
But I never locked anything, couldn't, and now pictures in gold frames
make my desk an address. Lonely, but an honorable solitude, and after all,
the one I asked for, the one I really married. Saying, I do,

and meaning, when I go, I will miss you most.

When I go, I will miss you most.
Swallowtails float hush-hush blue among trumpet vine. I chose fuchsia
for perfection, knowing well the pitfalls of excellence. Bells ring
into secrets known only to the Lyre snake that slid
among the rabbit's and ate
a new one. How is this about staying? How is this about a past life?
Danger lurks in the incipient flood and I don't entirely conjure rains.
Human children and fish children form an archipelago
of silence I can walk across.
I plant gardens of morning glories and cannas; the daylilies I left,
are in bloom right now, and someone sees them.
There, blue columbine and spiky blossom of the rampant chive need
cutting back. What is it about lost gardens
that they hurt like failed surgeries?
We cannot excise the scent of rosemary, the corn in early tassel.
Slice tiny beginnings in the hard envelope of nasturtiums:
wishing it was harder to remember where we came from.

Wishing it was harder to remember where we came from,
it becomes easier to say Kaddish. Whether
God is silent today, or not; we listen. Still, I suspect
the skin of seeds will shift and swell in their tender graves
no matter what, and a woman carrying starts in Egyptian pots,
will memorize her father's face as they cross the Navesink
that last time, just before
she carries his ashes
here.
No, not the ashes. They are gone, become compost in another story.
Instead, she has a stone, his name hewn and years, 1926-2000,
the memory of his hands, stirring jelly into tea, across his mother's

breakfast table; then, the real last time, at LaGuardia, kissing her palms.
Blessed for the years ahead without him. Say I'm from there.

Say I'm from there: the edges of paper, 13 wingspans of disappearance,
from trill of mimed resound, from the one that cannot be mated.
From swan's cry and peacock's cry, garlands and the strummed *vina*,
from clouds that shed no rain, but scent the day with coastal sweet.
From the unread last page, the dry eye over onions diced,
walks not taken, even when asked.
There are subjunctive verbs in Spanish for this,
says the woman who has married well, into an old family of some wealth,
that say what we intend more kindly; but I don't know them yet.
Si, si, I answer, meaning if, if. But you hear, Yes.
That's how love's echo works: a mistaken code for consent.
From fallen feathers, maybe, maybe not,
who could know, this life such a mystery except
where we go back, to motherlove, when I consider her light.

When I consider her light brought into this world, this way:
swung in, in a verdant garden, to Aretha's wail and us,
hopeful, waiting for the throes, to know her near. Dearly did she come,
rushing,
tiny rocket, ready for anything, hell-bent on joy.
How beauty does as beauty is, in this way,
simple; a give and give back to love.
Holy, clung to, each memory, each moment;
first-glimpse-moon in evening sky,
and the starshine that, it turns out, her eyes echo,
returned as gift . She is gift, Originalwise.
Tribune of GoddessMagicking invented her, mixed
bass and drum, stagelit grace, jeté and relevé,
vertebrate strength. Wish her love in the night kitchen, good dishes

from all the Mother's,
shelves of crystal, a closet of shoes: ruby slippers; to bring her
always home.

Always home to my heart, where secret, I keep you, Beloved.
Let us sleep outside tonight, listen to rivers past running, or running
away from. I remember God's voice at last, Ha-Kol, say the prayers
known only to the mockingbird, whose earnest echoes say,
come home, home,
where the heart is, not framed on a desk, but first bloom,
and quiet airports.
No one leaves, ever. Births danced for in gardens of early tomatoes, sweet,
daughters and fathers, and now this, sudden love and love left.
What was I thinking? Did I forget the feathers fallen
'round the Bosque, last light,
and the darkened moon that shone on scenery Turner would have painted,
if he hadn't loved clouds more. Come clear at long last, as landscape does:
tiny trumpet flower and the wild *tomatillo*.
Bougainvilleas flourish in any soil, and *Alcatraz*,
is here, a lily. A town tilted, but incandescent. Seeds become roots.
Propose that I stay: to the marriage of true minds, say yes.

Gift Event

Fill blue glass bottles with sparkling water and watch the air
travel for 3 timed minutes.

Give everyone brooms and new shoes to match.

Cook a pot of beans from the last harvest and give it
to the first person you see.

Don't take no for an answer.

Calibrate the distance from your elbow to the tip
of your middle finger in inches.

Write that many Love letters to the Invisible.

Stand outside near water and memorize a way to move like a river exactly.

Don't give up until you are downstream of yourself.

HERE IS YOUR SCARAB,

Jung said,
in the dream I did not have.

Gardens appeared.
I moved by bract and stem,
tasted the effervescent Divine in stamen and stutter.
Such green as I know is mine by birthright and the divination of dark roses.
My polar opposite is the sorrow of clouds,
the repeat of sky on lake skin.

Carried this, and only this, a memory,
also not mine,
to the mouth of Duck River,
to the sandstone Arches of Escalante, to the corner
of tomorrow, thru Tuesdays,
up to the edge of calamity and amnesia.

I abscond with other's memories; mine are too hard, too heavy,
I must put them down.
Have to.

I wrap my heart away in an orange shawl, embroidered with the names of
the ones
I must forget. Silk handwoven by Taurig women,
whose men ride camels
through the sands of Moroccan desert, in shrouds of moonlight.

I know these men, their eyes above shuttered faces, their story told
by the next generation.

A story of vanish and water's edge.
Of fabric and mystery.

Some fragrance takes over when words fall away.

I follow that, and the alembic of silence fires me into compassion,
marries me to golden osmanthus flower, found, only here,
on a Tennessee riverbank, in a humidity so costly
I can't afford its moist embrace.

In the treble notes of lemon myrtle,
        I infuse disappearance with roibois, and African Honeybush.
Sip the forgotten ambush of flavor,
of caravan and feast.

Become gypsy again, read my own palm, it says, "Practice".

Map to (W)holy Here

edged in crimson flowers, names I almost know,
unfurl on my tongue. Their fragrance, tangible and declamatory,
urgent somehow. *Casitas*, *azul*, and peach, sherbet colors, tangerine, lime.

I want to knock on each gated entry.

Elaborate doorways, like fancy buttons, that might just this second,
open, reveal
mysterious welcome.

Barely glimpsed, this coming
to
steep and sudden drop, trickster turns,
precipitous vertical. The etiquette of narrow passage,
every curb algebraic, a calculated risk.

I ought to have known. Everyone said.
I wouldn't listen, a passion for vertigo and volute.
Just go, I thought, and did.

I become the woman with everything: an ex-husband, an ex-country.
Egrets across her morning, constellations in fresh array,
Skywise, I am doing well, constantly Venus and Pleiades.
A galaxy of my own.

The riddle of streets is solved by secret courtyards, their private flourish,
plumbago and vivid bottle brush, wash on the line, canna lilies,
moss on stone.
The moist underpinnings of tropical:

tin cans gone botanical, geranium and trumpet honeysuckle,
everywhere garden, horticultural bedlam!

Outsider, I peak in, spy on shrines and shine, altars and roses,
lace camisoles,
Perpetual laundry.
Entreaties and La Vírgen, candles always burning.

I burn as well, would wish for things, if I only knew
what of all this beauty rumpus I wanted,
Or the language to ask in.

I pray in broken Spanish.
Pay in dreams with pesos and poetry,
buy green glass balls for the garden yet to grow,
cazuelas glazed in cobalt blue, sundrenched yellow:
a pattern of agave and swans. I crave luster, plates and pottery,
desire set after set of dishes, glassware, a bed of curliqued iron,
Everywhere lured by something new to eat,
tantalizing sizzle, *cebollas asada*, satin liquados of fresas and guava.

I shop, start collections; small balls of multicolored straw, votives of every
size and saint, warm honey and tiny mushrooms, blenders and buckets,
bouquets of spoons, and tuberoses.

I need Mercado 12 Step: Hello, I'm Judyth, and I haven't purchased a thing
for an hour.

Scarves of glittery thread, unimaginable shoes: blatant, operatic.

There are seraphim and cherubs everywhere,
a paradise of buslines, clang and clamor, I could travel all day, and never

have a clue
when I have arrived.

Corn tassels in English, in my new homelife,
relative and intimate. Something, at last, I think I know.

I shake the pollen, as ever,
thinking, salted water,
butter and sweet.
I make soup with blossoms of calabacitas, bought
walking the cobbled streets, pressed into my hands,
and accepted.

How gala our daily life, flowers become feast!
Each nearly understood moment!

Slowly, become bilingual in *frijoles verdes y tomates,*
Albacahar y salvia.
Translate into jasmine, trumpet vines staked to rock wall.

Morning glories, Heavenly Blue, seek a hold, climb, and bloom.
I study them, *memorize this*, I think.

I live somewhere I never expected,
that understands *barbacoa,* is versed in *queso,*
fluent in *tamale* and *atole.*
Learn *carnitas* and *tomatillo.*
Every meal served blessed, every stranger, greeted,
Conjugate morning, afternoon and night.

I also speak daughter
elsewhere, and infrequent

news, No Tzatziki and schmooz.

I took Greek so for granted: who knew I would need a talisman
of stuffed grape leaves,
an oracle of spanikopita and moussaka, baba ghanouj
and the constant voices of my children.

There is a map, and I unfold
along set creases. Discover a walk,
ancient, and tender, palms held open,
move by scent and savor.
Track angels,
Think dragons.

Send postcards: *Having
a wonderful time.*

Wish you

DON'T TRAVEL, JOURNEY!

Take a vacation from the human world.
From your own history,
With its tedious invective, its distortions,
Its endless cups of coffee gone cold on your desk.

Go where something you do not suspect,
or even hope for,
is waiting.
Has been waiting. Was always.

This minute invent patience, name a painting,
Eat a fruit the color of tomorrow, wear Lila Dow's
voice like a fringed shawl: cover yourself in *corridas*.

Forget the mother you think you had,
The one that didn't do it right.
Whose did? Did I,
with my precious chance?

Retell your story.
Start where the jasmine entwines so delicate in air,
Sends fragrance freely across the kitchen's open door.

Go outside. Let your story be mountain and sweet Acacia in bloom,
the lily's re-born white cup.
Grow up from winter sleep with the Canna and the wild blue sage.

You can wear the fresh face of flowers.
Be the puckered envelope of new roses,

The start of bougainvillea, beloved sneeze of Jacaranda.

Centro is all decked out in plumbago;
You would look so good in that shade of lavender,
Stunning on you, wouldn't your mother say,
in this version.

StudioOnlySymbolHearsWindDesire

Poems are made daily, with small tools, in the studio.
Bocelli sings love songs in soft Italian, as if only
he knew to call to the Goddess by voice, and not symbol.
When no one speaks, does it mean no one hears?
I send entreaties and gratitude on the wind.
This hope is sheer masquerade, I am drowning in Desire.

Every morning I wake with Desire
to be in my studio,
then a different wind
blows through my day and only
the Angel hears
my work. What used to be real becomes just symbol

of a symbol.
The Buddha said all suffering is rooted in Desire.
Temple bells ring us to work, and the earthworm alone hears
or listens: the ground, with its multitude of seeds is his studio.
And his only
music is wind.

I listen with joy to that wind.
The Chinese ideogram for happiness is a symbol
that gives us not only
Desire
but the grasses that lay down in surrender on the way to Cezanne's studio.
Make the declarative sentence Hemingway hears.

The Completed One hears
the rustling of oak leaves in the wind
stirring ashes in the sculptor's abandoned studio.
The Crone Priestess of Dodana sends out the black dove, not symbol
but the way we summon the oracle of Desire.
If you say one thing more, say only

it is a door for moonlight, to tell what only
Moonlight hears.
That is the beautymaker's real Desire:
to send out work on the wind.
Broken lines form the symbol
for wholeness: this sends us always into the studio.

Go gladly into your studio. This is the only
way we move from symbol into the listening that hears
stories carried for centuries, on the caravan wind of our Desire.

Ritual for the Wild Love Moon

1. Know what is shining.
2. Name it.
3. Compose a letter to that light.
4. Address an envelope to the Ripe, the Seeded One, Voluptuous Olive, and mail with a blue stamp.
5. Plant seeds of round fruits.
6. Make a white corn tortilla.
7. Know what comes over you so suddenly.
8. Write sorrow, eggplant, sacred jimson, on your left palm, and clap 3 times.
9. Cover all the mirrors with green silk and honeysuckle vine.
10. Eat the tortilla.

Everything Is In Front Of Us

When I stop speaking,
this poem
will open its wings.

Take the palomino's reins, turn his head toward town,
where the welcoming dead feast on honey's clovered translation.

The meadow calls to us in vine, in leaves
going so gently—yellow.

Look in the mirror, and be seen by infinite varieties of light.

This rose, this outcry of swallow's flight—
What wings do we wear at journey's end?
See the road, see it?

Stop in certainty there,
Praising the vivid harvest.
Prairies stretch before us in the reverie of bells,
in the play of chime and destined ring.

Toll, toll. Ache for an understanding of thorns,
the pierce of fragrance.

On this map, learn the latitude of angels.

Memorize the latticed patterns of coral.
Clamor for the overhead passing of the Perseid,
become egrets by morning.

Sit your heart where your mind is.
Speak from underneath
the buddleia, butterfly bush, when

those leaves fall,
watch for wings everywhere.

LOVE'S OFFICES

What did I know, what did I know
—Robert Hayden

Love with its featherweight measure
With its a e i o u
With its why of the cry of the falcon, of the beloved in the dark,
the dredged riverbottom of bedtalk.
Love with its calling from centuries,
with its clock of barely moving hands in the plaza of Perugia,
Love with its tiny steps
and kimonos sleeves wet with walking in the morning garden.
Love with its capacity for rhyme
And drift. Love with its backward glance
And endless coffee.
Love with its heat lightening and all night itch
Love with its red red wine
and bad driving, hillsides of pine and honeysuckle tango.
Love with its stone Buddha
 in the almond scented light.
Love with its too long sentences and fierce electric.
Love with its armchairs of desire, and groceries of tomatoes, fresh basil,
garlic and olives. Love with its redundancy of salad and lack of pizza.
Love with its piano teeth, and islands of soft winds,
the Southern Cross at midnight, and mangos mangos mangos.
Love with its dire relationship to roses and thirst
Love with its Catalpa trees and unfought wars
Love with its chrysanthemum eyes and velvet skin
with its leopard eyes and slow discovery of other music.
Love, o love with its Rothko eyes, and Brancusi hands

And vintner's tongue and champagne tongue.
Love, thief and scholar,
giver and gift.
The dreaming we leave behind at the moist blue end,
the dream we wake from, tender, each morning.

Thanking Andre Breton, for Free Union....

Oficinas del amor

Qué supe, qué supe
—Robert Hayden

Amor con su medida peso pluma
Con su a e i o u
Con su por qué del grito del halcón, del bienamado en la oscuridad,
la dragada orilla del río de la charla de cama.
Amor con su llamado de siglos,
con su reloj de manos que apenas se mueven en la plaza de Perugia,
Amor con sus pequeños pasos
y mangas de kimonos mojadas con caminatas en el jardín de la mañana.
Amor con su capacidad de rima
Y derivar. Amor con su mirada hacia atrás
Y café sin final.
Amor con su calor brillante y comezón toda la noche
Amor con su rojo rojo vino
y mal manejo, laderas de tango de pino y madreselva.
Amor con su piedra de Buda
en la luz con esencia de almendra.

Amor con sus enunciados demasiado largos y feroz eléctrico.
Amor con sus sillones de deseo y sus abarrotes de tomates, albahaca fresca,
ajo y aceitunas. Amor con su redundancia de salado y falta de pizza.
Amor con sus teclas de piano, e islas de vientos suaves,
la Cruz del Sur a medianoche, y mangos mangos mangos.
Amor con sus funestas relaciones para rosas y sed
Amor con sus árboles de Catalpa y guerras sin pelearse
Amor sus ojos de crisantemo y piel de terciopelo
con sus ojos de leopardo y lento descubrimiento de otra música.

Amor, o amor con sus ojos Rothko, y manos Brancusi
Y lengua de vinatero y lengua champaña.
Amor, ladrón y escolar
dador y regalo.
El soñar que dejamos detrás en el húmedo final azul
El sueño del que despertamos, tierno, cada mañana.

Gracias André Breton, por Unión Libre

Translation by
Selene González

Wisteria Mantra

Stick with your tenderness.
The mantra of sweet incubates into a future of spin and giggle.

Stick around.
From here the view is good, the hour always nearing lunch,
Torta Cubana con pico de gallo, or
Milanesa?

Wisteria in luxurious drape, lavish.
Nearly lucid, textual arbor. Take it as read,
Blooming.

Resilient lavender. Flowers in tender translation to scent,
kindled by light:
the mantra of fish.

Stick with fish.
Swim flickerwise into morning
And be caught by circumstance and ripple.

Stick with incubate, grow yourself into language,
a heart for all seasons, wisdom of clouds,
dispensing at their ease.

Stick with mantra.
Repeat: joyful water joyful water joyful water.

Startled Solstice

Ask for an emerald belt,
hung with home tools, peacemakers:
wooden spoon, string of pearls,
basket of wild rush and hummingbird feathers.

Ask for the waters of resolution,
sea sponge of re-awaken.

Exchange your sackcloth for verdigris spandex,
Cut low over the kidneys,
let your curves have voice and belly bell out,
exchange breath with candlelight:
burn in and out slowly.

Suddenly you are entirely jasmine,
Blooming as never before,
Valley turned tumult of bright,
Bougainvillea and wild white poppy,
Air a fine vintage, sparkling, and slightly acidic,
Scent of acacia and *amor seco.*

Tell stories on hectares of corn, ox plowed,
Scythed into rampant lush, burrofest come fall.

Make your heart an infusion for the Beloved to sip,
Make thirst be as lips to cup, as stars strewn across fish net
Don't take a ruler to the need to belong together –
Use eons, use raspberries,

There is no ledger sheet in love.

Stir profit and loss until the heat of spin and sunder

turn into powder and dissolve.
Throw the switch on the erotic circuit:
That's the secret of marine phosphorescence,
Water gone sweet, enrobe us,
pure bonbon, in depths of fallen light.

Considering surface,
cast a serpent on the waters -
You'll be the lucky one, rolling over in the morning from dream
into those freckled arms!
Say: What makes me dive in headfirst,
Meaning: Refractory pattern of calcite bring us to color twice over.

Drench us into life, O Isis,
Xochiquetzal, ignite us into pleasure,
honeysuckle sweet, sharp as sensual grassblade -
Dakinis, take us to winds extreme,
Lilith, paint us into our darkness,
Gaia, Ala, Izanami, send us to seed, seeking light,
Brigid of the Wells, may we be wriggle and liquefy,
Numi, teach us to shed skin, re-claim freshet and seep.

When the knight asks what ails you,
answer with the health of turned earth,
the thresher's song this minute.

Wear the Ring of the New

Cosmos bloom vivid on our Boulevard of Sweet,
MoonWheel turns 13 times round,
journey's end marries journeys begun.
This road leads from Yes to Yes!

A year, a world, a life, is honied and new.
Freshmade from the Old, the recipe is simple:
 paper water trumpet vine
A musical note, sustained in the key of Bee,
the canyon buzzzzzzzzzz is Kiss and Bless!
Let's borrow the blue from a canopy of sky,
braid our DNA into the Fibonacci of sunflowers.

Everything starts now, and here:
to seed is the whole thing!
Let's promise to serve and conserve:
make a holy jam of berries!
Have a crush on grapes!

Corn tassels at the speed of bliss.
Tomatoes practice the economy of blush: Such a deal!
We'll make a cottage industry of beauty,
give the butterflies a raise,
Retire to a bed of zinnias.

At the heart of garden, sister to sister, frijoles, calabacitas;
Shhh, the chisme is *Ripen*, whispered ear to ear!
The secret's out: Flowers big as dinner plates!

This life a feast! Que viva, L'Chaim!
Earth so Divine! Let's live here!

Close your eyes and open your mouth-
The flavor of happiness is on your lips:
Delicious you!
Joy is this kingdom of today...
Another year inscribed in the Book of Life!
How easy to love how it is,
how everything we love just is.

WAGE PEACE

Wage peace with your breath.

Breathe in firemen and rubble,
breathe out whole buildings and flocks of red wing blackbirds.

Breathe in terrorists
and breathe out sleeping children and freshly mown fields.

Breathe in confusion and breathe out maple trees.

Breathe in the fallen and breathe out lifelong friendships intact.

Wage peace with your listening: hearing sirens, pray loud.

Remember your tools: flower seeds, clothes pins, clean rivers.

Make soup.

Play music, memorize the words for thank you in three languages.

Learn to knit, and make a hat.

Think of chaos as dancing raspberries,
imagine grief
as the outbreath of beauty
or the gesture of fish.

Swim for the other side.

Wage peace.

Never has the world seemed so fresh and precious:

Have a cup of tea and rejoice.

Act as if armistice has already arrived.
Celebrate today.

Last Time

Say coyote and mean surprise.
Say fallen petals and mean the way you look at me.
Say *espinaca* and mean the color leaves learn at birth.
Say doorway and mean a courtyard from memory.
Say chocolate and mean little Buddha in the mouth.
Say Febrero and mean first scent of sweet acacia on the wind.

When we are gone say lemon tree, say new buds, say palm fronds,
And mean that you loved it here.
Say *maguey* and mean thorny guardians of the heart.

Say mesquite and mean the rattle of later.
Say that twice and mean the rattle heard over long distances of night alone.
Say stars falling, and don't mean that.
Say fish in the quiet pond and mean early rain.

Say starfish and I can't tell you what that means.
Say cloud and mean a dream that wakes you.
Say glass table and mean the first step on a journey.
Say tamales and mean kalamata olives.
Say I will give you what I have brought and mean voice.
Say doorway again and see what it means.
Say look one more time and mean thank you.

Author Bios

aaron a. abeyta was born and raised in the San Luis Valley of southern Colorado.

He has published three books, *colcha*, *As Orion Falls*, and *Rise, Do Not be Afraid*.

aaron received his MFA from Colorado State University. He now works as a professor of English at Adams State University.

For his book, colcha, aaron received the 2002 American Book Award and the 2001 Colorado Book Award. His most recent book, *Rise, Do Not be Afraid*, was a finalist for the 2007 Colorado Book Award. In 1998 he won the Colorado Council on the Arts Fellowship for Poetry. Other awards include a first prize from the American Academy of Poets, for his poem "colcha," and a grand prize winner of CSU's Creative and Performing Arts Scholarship.

aaron has work published in 'An Introduction to Poetry, 10th ed.,' Literature: An Introduction to Fiction, Poetry, & Drama, 8th ed.' 'The Dry Creek Review,' 'Sage Plains Review,' 'Chokecherries,' 'Colorado Central Magazine' and various other journals.

Tani Arness currently resides in Albuquerque, New Mexico. She grew up in rural Poulsbo, Washington, surrounded by water and cedar trees, before moving to the desert. The beauty of nature has always been a refuge for her and plays an important part in her creative work. For more than a decade, Tani travelled in over thirty countries, finding inspiration in the people and places she discovered. In her writing, Tani often finds herself exploring themes of place, and more recently, delving into themes of spirituality, femininity and beauty.

Tani loves learning and has been a teacher for many years. She taught in schools in rural Shamva, Zimbabwe and Wales, Alaska before settling in New Mexico. Since completing her master's in creative writing at the University of New Mexico, Tani continues to study, teach, and write. Tani currently teaches poetry at a charter high school created for "at-risk" students.

For the past fifteen years, Tani has been part of a writing group called Glorious. She is eternally grateful for the support, insight, commitment and playfulness of these women and the space they create. Each day Tani dedicates herself to beauty and spirit. Each day she opens herself to the surprising expanse of creativity in the intersection of words and living.

Tani's prose and poetry can be found in numerous literary magazines including *North American Review*, *Red Rock Review*, *Green Mountains Review*, *Adobe Walls*, *Malpais*, and *Crab Orchard Review*. She is currently working on a full-length manuscript of poems tentatively titled, *Back to the Bible: Freeing the Feminine*.

Richard Broderick is the author of two collections of poetry, *Woman Lake* (New Rivers Press) and *Rain Dance* (Parallel Press), and *Night Sale* (New Rivers Press), a collection of short stories.

His poetry has appeared in numerous publications and anthologies, including *The Book of Irish-American Poetry from the Eighteenth Century to the Present* (University of Notre Dame Press). The recipient of a Minnesota State Arts Board Literary Fellowship and a Minnesota Book Award, he is a two-time winner of the Many Voices Project, and many other awards and honors for his poetry, including a full fellowship to the George Mason University MFA program, an International Merit Award from *Atlanta Review*, two nominations for the Pushcart Prize, and selection as a finalist for the Robert Frost Foundation Award.

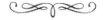

Judyth Hill is a poet, author and teacher, living on her Farm in a verdant, mountain-ringed valley outside San Miguel de Allende, Mexico.

Her eight published books of poetry include *Presence of Angels*, *Men Need Space*, *Black Hollyhock*, *First Light*, and her newest, *Dazzling Wobble*.

She is the author of the internationally acclaimed poem, *Wage Peace*, a recipient of many poetry grants & fellowships.

Hill conducts poetry workshops at writing conferences internationally, is the annual Poet-in-Residence at various schools in the United States, and teaches online, *www.judythhill.com*. In partnership with Chef Kris Rudolph, she leads WildWriting Culinary Adventures around the world, *www.eat-write-travel.com*.

She conducts on-going poetry and writing classes in San Miguel, and is the poetry editor of *SOL: English Writing in Mexico*, published online at *www.solliterarymagazine.com*.
She was described by the St. Helena Examiner as, "Energy with skin", and The Denver Post as, "A tigress with a pen".

Katherine DiBella Seluja is a nurse poet who is actively involved in transposing both personal and professional healthcare experiences into poetry and prose. She studied classical piano for 15 years of her childhood and attributes much of the lyricism and rhythm in her writing to this early musical training. Katherine holds degrees in Nursing from both Columbia University and Yale University. As many of those working in health care know, patients frequently become part of our own personal stories. Katherine invites these stories to inform her writing and strives to reveal raw and powerful aspects of health and illness in poetic and lyrical forms.

Katherine is also frequently inspired by her Italian heritage and stories that she heard from her grandparents. She lives in Santa Fe, New Mexico with her husband and two daughters. She can be found at *katherineseluja.com.*